VISIONS AND VISITORS

Memoir of a Psychic

VISIONS AND VISITORS

Memoir of a Psychic

≈

Susan Stockton

SYNCLECTIC MEDIA

Published by **Synclectic Media**

Seattle, Washington

www.synclectic.com

Publisher's Cataloging-in-Publication Data

Stockton, Susan

Visions and Visitors: Memoir of a Psychic / Susan Stockton.. – 1st ed.

p. cm. –

Summary: Visions and Visitors chronicles Susan's spiritual journey as an ordinary child whose startling gifts forced her to entertain the notion that she was birthed into an extraordinary life. She was raised in a devout Catholic family and schooled by religious nuns. This environment nurtured her visions and she soon realized that she possessed what her Irish ancestors called the gift of "second sight."

Susan intertwines the story of her inward struggle to become her authentic self, with the complexities of her daily life as wife, mother, single parent and breadwinner. Despite the conflict she felt about her choice of whether to follow a conventional career or embrace her gifts as a psychic medium, her "call to service" triumphs.

Library of Congress Control Number: 2014949769

ISBN: 9780692261644

[1. Spiritual Memoir—Nonfiction. 2. Autobiography—Nonfiction.] I. Title.

P-CIP

10 9 8 7 6 5 4 3 2

Ω

First Edition

Printed in the United States

To my children, Barry and Sheila
Who love me despite my choices.

To my sisters Ananfaye and Gloria who always support me.

10% of the publisher's proceeds from
Visions and Visitors: Memoir of a Psychic
will be donated to
The Breast Cancer Research Foundation
For more information visit www.bcrfcure.org

Thank you to everyone in my Tempe writing group for your helpful criticism—especially to our facilitator and my friend Shari Broyer for all her expertise, guidance and wise editing. I also thank my friends, other writers and my family who read the manuscript, made comments and gave me useful advice. Whether I heeded their advice or not, I always listened.

Blessed

Listening within
The soul beckons you to love
Celebrate blessed gifts.

~Annie Louise Balzanto

Thanks to my cousin Annie for her perfect expression of
Haiku that captures the spirit of my life's work.

Prologue

My first vision occurred when I was six, while on my way home from grammar school in Portland, Oregon. My older brother always ran ahead of me as we left the bus stop. Lagging behind, I knelt carefully on the cool dirt so as not to get my school uniform dirty. Nearby, a cluster of blue crocuses thrust themselves from their bed of moist earth toward the fading afternoon light that beamed through the trees. I knelt in prayer to the Blessed Virgin with my rosary in my hands. When I finished, I looked up to see the image of a woman commingled with the tree, her face clearly visible, the tree's yellow blossoms clustered about her head like a halo. Below, a large Oregon grapevine, heavy with leaves of variant greens, covered her feet. I recognized her from the statues I had seen in our church. It was Our Lady, Mary. She smiled at me. During her appearance, the sounds around me stopped, as did time. Today, I still believe that it was the Blessed Mother who came to me in my innocent prayers.

The visitations occurred regularly that year; the image of Our Blessed Mother always the same. They stopped when my sister Molly joined my brother and me on the bus ride, so we all walked home together and I was no longer alone.

I never mentioned these occurrences to anyone. I believe the apparitions were real, not the product of a devout child's imagination. I do know that I was destined to see and hear things others could not: voices of dead people calling to me; prophecies of the future; and scenes of the past--people dressed in the attire of bygone eras—like videos in my head.

Gilbert Arizona
March 15, 2013

"When I find myself in times of trouble, Mother Mary comes to me, speaking words of wisdom, let it be. . . The Beatles,"Let it Be."

Apple Records, released May 8, 1970

Part 1: KARMA

Chapter 1
1951 – Seattle, Washington: Second Sight

My mother's face drained of color and furrows wrinkled her high forehead. She stopped stirring with her wooden spoon and gazed into the cast iron roaster, thick with beef drippings that she was about to use to make gravy for Sunday dinner.

"Mom, what's the matter? What do you see?" I asked, giving a frightened shudder.

"Susan, its Robb. He's hurt. He can't hear or see anything; he's lying on a gravel road. He went through the windshield and someone's covering him with a blanket. Can't they hear him breathing? My God! Why can't the officers see that he's alive? Alive, do you hear me? Alive!" Mom spoke alternately to me and to the people she saw in the drippings.

"Your brother's the youngest of the lot, too. He doesn't even have his driver's license yet. He's alive, take off the blanket! Can't you see he's breathing? That danged policeman thinks he's dead. Where's the ambulance, the medics?"

Then my mother grew silent. Her vision was over; the spell was broken. She was left to her own fears, and I to my feelings of helplessness. Our dinner of roast beef and mashed potatoes sat waiting on the stovetop. She deftly skimmed off the fat, left the drippings in the roasting pan, and put the slab of beef on a large platter that she then sat on the kitchen countertop. Into the hot drippings, she blended flour and butter until they reached a grainy consistency, then added a touch of milk and emptied a large ladle of water taken from the potatoes that boiled on the stove into the mix. Her voice steadied, and in soft tones she said to me, "Susan, see how it's done? Stir the mixture constantly or the gravy will be lumpy, and drain the fat well in the beginning or else the gravy will be too greasy."

I took the spoon from my mother's hand and made circular motions with it, watching the mixture turn as smooth and glossy as the paint in a newly-opened can. Hoping my mother would be pleased by the transition I'd made from fat and flour to silky gravy, I looked up to see her face frozen in the expression she'd worn earlier, when she first saw something in the drippings. My apprehension intensified, and I found myself holding my breath.

Finally, Mom turned off the stove, drained the water from the potatoes, seasoned the potatoes—adding milk, butter, salt and pepper—and handed me the masher. Slowly, I exhaled. Then, abruptly, she raced from the kitchen, the words tumbling off her lips, "Dear God, what have I seen? Jesus, Mary and Joseph, you'd think I was a gypsy fortuneteller scrying into a crystal ball! Lord Jesus, I can't even stop it while I cook! God Almighty, let it be my imagination! Only, God in Heaven knows, it never is."

I knew something terrible was happening, but I mashed the potatoes. I had learned not to ply my mother with questions when she was seeing things I couldn't see.

Twenty minutes later, she was in the dining room speaking with Daddy in low tones when the kitchen telephone rang. I grabbed the receiver off the hook to hear a gruff voice ask, "Mrs. Stockton?"

"No," I answered. "May I ask who's calling?"

"Officer Svensen, Highway Patrol, King County," he replied.

My voice began to quiver as I shouted into the phone, "Just a minute, Officer, I'll get her." I turned away to call, "Mom! Dad! A Highway Patrol officer is on the phone."

"I knew it, I *knew* it!" My mother's voice wailed through the house.

My dad grabbed the phone from me. "Yes, Officer?" he said.

"Mr. Stockton? Do you have a fifteen-year-old-son named Robert?" I heard the officer ask as my father put the receiver to his ear.

"Yes, Robert is my son... No. We can drive to the hospital ourselves... He's unconscious? ...An auto accident?"

"Bob, what is it?" my mom called out, but she already knew the answer to her question.

Daddy turned to me and stroked my long copper-colored hair. "That's my good girl, Susan," he said. "You're in middle school. You're old enough to be in charge, and I know you can handle it." I was after all the oldest of the girls. "If any of the other boys' parents call, let them know that we're on our way to King County Hospital and that the boys got into an accident on their way home from the drag races. Tell them that's all you know."

Now my father spoke to all of us. He asked Molly to help with Margie and baby Reenie (Noreen). He said that Robb was seriously injured and that he would call us from the hospital when he had more information. He suggested that we eat our dinner and clean up afterward, as usual.

"Maybe you could all say the rosary especially for Robb before you go to bed." My father leaned down to give each of us a quick kiss, and I looked around for Mom, but she was already out the door, standing in the driveway waiting for Daddy to come and unlock the car door. As he talked, my stomach churned with anxiety, as well as from hunger from the smell of roast beef that wafted into the living room. Daddy grabbed his jacket from the coat closet and called out his "leaving home" mantra, "Susan, Molly, Margie, guard baby Reenie with your lives!"

When they left, I stood at the head of the table and actually managed to carve the rare roast into thin slices the way my dad did even though my hands still shook with the shock of hearing about my brother's accident.

Molly said grace, "Bless us, oh Lord, for these, thy gifts, which we are about to receive. Amen."

I was fretting inside. My sisters could see me faltering and would have no small talk.

"Susan, is Robbie going to die?" Molly asked.

"No Molly. I think Robb will be alright. Daddy will call us."

Margie began to cry, asking between sobs, "Is his face smashed up? Can he breathe?"

"Honestly, he will be alright."

"How do you know, Susan?"

"I just know."

I dished up their plates, adding carrots, Brussels sprouts, and spooning gravy over the mashed potatoes and succulent roast beef.

"Margie, we don't need you acting like a crybaby right now, for heaven's sake! Robb's not going to die," Molly scolded.

The meal ended, and I scrubbed down the Formica counters. Molly washed dishes, Margie dried and we all put them away. I swept the floor and took out the garbage just as the schedule of our chores, taped to the fridge, decreed.

Then we prayed, kneeling in a circle in the living room.

The phone rang as we finished the last "Our Father" of the last decade of the rosary. "...we forgive those who trespass against us, and lead us not into temptation but deliver us from evil. Amen."

I turned to my sisters with the comforting news, "Girls, Robb will be alright. Mom and Daddy are staying with him for awhile, and he's going to be fine. He has a concussion, but he's conscious now, and they'll know more in the morning when the specialist goes over the results of the tests."

We busied ourselves getting the little ones to bed. Molly warmed Reenie a bottle of milk. She loved to put the baby to bed and sing her Mom's favorite Irish lullaby, "Too ra loo ra loo, too ra loo ra lai, hush now don't you cry. Over in Killarney many years ago, me mither sang a song to me..."

I tried to distract Margie by helping her brush her teeth and put on her nightgown. I sat on the edge of her bed stroking her forehead and running my fingers through her curly hair, speaking to her in soft tones to coax her into sleep.

Later, after Molly and I were in our beds, I lay under my covers, relieved by the quiet, but exhausted from the strain of the last few hours, worrying. What if something happened to Robb, and I no longer had a big brother? I'd never felt responsible for Robb like I did my younger sisters. Robb was different. It was more likely he felt responsible for me, since he always protected me. We had a strong bond.

I cried silently so Molly, in her bunk bed below me, wouldn't hear me. I imagined how scary it must have been to go flying through a windshield and land on a gravel road. Did Robb remember the accident? I prayed to God that He would help Robb get well, fast.

Snuggled in bed, eyes closed, I saw again my mother's face as she looked into the pan on the stove. I recalled knowing my grandfather was going to die because I had seen him lying in a coffin in a dream. My cousin, Honora, and I giggled while our mothers wept in the strange dream. We laughed so loud that we had to run out of the funeral parlor while the family said the rosary for him. I never told my mom about the dream because she loved her father dearly, and it would have made her sad. Yet, when Grandpa died soon afterwards, I was frightened.

Alarmed at the memory, I dug further down under the layers of blankets piled over me. "I guess I see things like my mother does," I whispered into the dark. I was only twelve; I didn't want to see things.

Chapter 2
1951 – Empaths

"Mom baked me chocolate chip cookies when you were at school today," Robb announced from the living room. I had come in from school and was scurrying to change from my uniform into pedal-pushers and a t-shirt so I could go outside and ride my bike.

My brother had taken weeks to recuperate from his auto accident. He stayed home from school and Mom doted on him, as we all tended to do since the accident.

"Guess who signed my leg cast today? The best-looking girl in our high school came over at lunchtime to visit me. Her dad let her drive his car. Sue, look at the way she scrawled her name—Sandy—on my cast." He grinned at me, eyes twinkling.

"Robb, you're such a tease! Did Sandy really come to visit you? She's a cheerleader. That's so groovy," I joked, relieved. I had been consumed with fear that my idol would somehow be different, or get sick, or his constant headaches since the accident would worsen.

When we had played "kick-the can" in the alley behind our new home in Seattle, Robb defended me if the older boys on the block played too rough. He'd call out to me, "Sis, follow me! We can hide together in the thick of the blackberry patch." He was daring, and I wanted to be like him, but instead I was all too often stuck with my sisters and the other neighborhood girls. I tagged along with him as much as he'd allow it.

Now, in an effort to get on his good side and make him feel better, I offered to loan him some of my babysitting money. I usually didn't let him borrow from me because he took too long to pay it back.

9

Robb guffawed, "Loaning me money, that's a first! Ha, ha! It took an accident to get money out of you! Thanks. How about I buy some model airplanes to work on while I'm home from school? Sis, you've been great."

I blushed at the rare compliment from my big brother.

Molly joined us, and I couldn't keep the excitement out of my voice. Changing the subject, I said, "I'm so looking forward to high school in a few months! I'll make new friends, take the trip into the city every day, and go to parties and dances, too!"

I prattled on to Molly as Robb went back to reading his *Hot Rod* magazine. Molly took in every word I said because she'd soon follow me to high school and she wanted to know everything I knew.

My mother entered the living room and began scolding us. "You two have been over at the Casey's again, haven't you?"

Dumbfounded that she knew about it, we nevertheless shook our heads "no." We'd definitely been playing with the Casey girls even though Mom had forbidden it. I had parked my bike up the road, and Molly had snuck down the alley to knock on their basement door. We'd spent the whole afternoon enjoying ourselves with them.

Molly said now, continuing our earlier conversation, "Will you still share a bedroom with me Susan, when you go off to high school? I'm going to public school, or maybe to the new Catholic co-ed school, Blanchett," she declared.

"Of course we'll share. Where else would I sleep? Hopefully not with the babies! I like being in the room with you and being able to talk about things with you before we go to sleep."

Mother interrupted us again, annoyed that we had lied to her. "I told you two not to hang out with those girls! Susan, you're sounding just like them, using bad grammar with a twang in your voice. And stop flicking your hair the way Kate does! Molly, you're using that flippant tone of voice they all use in that house and I see you've changed your hair so you look like their youngest. Now tidy up in here, and don't lie to me when I can easily tell where you've been!"

I didn't think I was speaking like my friends, but my mother's ability to tell what we'd been up to stemmed from much, more than simple observation, as I realized by the time I graduated from high school. My mother was an empath. She could *feel* where we'd been. It took me a long time to understand that. It took even longer to comprehend that Molly and I were also empaths, and that, as highly sensitive girls, we had the ability to read our friends' thoughts and scan their psyches for feelings. In doing so, we unconsciously picked up their traits, habits and mannerisms. I came to understand that being an empath has both biological and spiritual aspects and is genetic, is inherent in our DNA, and is passed on from generation to generation.

Summer passed, and Robb was well again. My first day of high school was nigh, and I lay in bed thinking of tomorrow when I would ride the bus with my dad into Seattle, joining him on his daily commute to the office where he worked. The plan was that I would continue on to Capitol Hill to my Catholic all girls' high school.

I had made a pact with myself that I would no longer be the shy, quiet girl, the studious teacher pleaser I'd always been; instead, I'd make friends immediately, and that meant I'd have to reach out to new people. If I waited for others to approach me, I might never make friends.

With that idea in mind, I dreamed of a grownup life. I would wear lipstick—if Mom would let me—and put my long auburn hair in a ponytail. I'd also buy new sweaters and skirts for all the dances I planned to attend. I was determined to have lots of girlfriends and a boyfriend, if possible. If I babysat enough, I'd be able to earn money for an angora—or possibly cashmere—twin sweater set, maybe not the first year, but definitely by the time I was a sophomore.

During our commute into Seattle, Daddy told me stories of his time in the Marianna Islands when he was in the Navy and also of his childhood days in Oklahoma and Missouri.

"Sue, as a member of the Armed Services during World War II in the South Pacific islands, I had to live with people from all over the United States. Some of them didn't believe in God, others had never had a loving family and would do anything for love. I realized then what a great set of parents I had. I know now how lucky I am to be loved by your mom and you kids. My mother, your grandmother Stockton, took care of me and gave me the gift of strong faith, especially after my dad died. The Navy taught me a lot about the world. Not everyone will think like you do. You might be tempted to let others influence you, but stay true to the values you've learned at home."

"Now Sue," he continued, "you'll have plenty of opportunities to make friends, so choose them wisely. You'll likely remember these high school days all your life as they'll determine what you do in the future, even more so than college."

Daddy showed me where to transfer to the downtown bus that would take me straight to my new school. He hugged and kissed me goodbye and walked toward his office in the Smith Tower. With my bus transfer in hand, I thought about what he'd told me, and I felt happy that I'd been able to talk with him about life. I cherished our time together and felt grown up.

I skipped along 18th Street toward the brick church with its imposing 150-foot, Italianate, twin bell towers built of old growth timber. Each tower was topped with a zinc-coated cross and ball. Inside the church, thick wood timbers from the area had been used for the enormous pews. I only caught the end of the Mass on that first day of school but realized that if I could come earlier, I could attend mass and communion in this famous church beside my school every day.

The steps up to the school were long and steep. Stopping on the landing, I decided to talk with the first person who looked friendly. A girl with long, honey blonde hair that hung in curls around her shoulders kept looking around as if she didn't know which of the two huge doors she should open to go into the school. I reached out to pull open the door to my right and she followed me in. Janet was a freshman like me. My new friend smiled at me, and I knew I belonged.

As I waited for the teacher to come to my assigned classroom, I could hardly sit still in my chair. High school was so nifty! Sister Mary Sheila, a petite young nun with a wide smile, opened her mouth to greet us and, by the end of the day, she was everyone's favorite.

Sister Sheila outlined all the rules, "Girls, there will be no lipstick of any kind on the premises, or on your mouths. Hair must be combed neatly and held securely with a clip or barrettes. No rubber bands in your hair, which means there will be no ponytails. Uniforms are to be worn with nylon hose and dark shoes. No bobby socks, ever. Also, there must be no talking in the halls between classes."

The uniforms weren't hip or trendy by anyone's standards. They were navy blue dresses with long sleeves made of serge and had flared skirts, fitted waists and bodices. White cotton detachable collars fit around the neck. The nuns considered them quite smart-looking. My only consolation was that I was as thin as a celery stick and could wear the fitted dress well. Robb had often teased me as I walked around the house, "Sue, when you walk across the hardwood planks on the living room floor, be careful you don't fall through the cracks!" I didn't think his joke was funny since I was self-conscious about my skinny, boyish body.

What I hated most from Sister's litany of rules was that we couldn't wear lipstick or pull our hair back into ponytails, even though we all had very long hair. How mortifying this was, especially when we already had to wear uniforms. We couldn't hide on the city bus but had to sit with all the chic girls from Garfield High. When the bell rang and we were done for the day, we soon learned to pull out our lipsticks, find our stash of rubber bands, and brush our hair into ponytails.

Janet and I bought lunch that first day of school and ate together. We walked down the street to a snack shop owned by a creepy old Chinese man who kept staring at us while we ate. I had never been gone all day from home, except during camp or at a relative's house, and I felt sophisticated and important to be able to buy my own lunch.

During the long ride back to suburbia that evening, I tried to say the names of my new classmates. "Hirabayashi, Dravojevich, Guerin, Goudeau, and Pioli," I repeated to myself. The familiar surnames of Woods, Murphy and Kerr were like mine, while strange names of the girls with faces of color made me feel pale and different with my copper hair.

Experiences I did not know about until later had forged these girls' lives in ways I could not fathom. I felt empathetic when I learned my classmates' stories, and the diversity that surrounded me changed my worldview.

Lilly Dravojevich was so beautiful, with her long curly hair and angelic face, that I couldn't believe her family was numbered among the 200,000 refugees who had fled their country during the Hungarian revolution before the Soviets invaded in 1956. Or that another sweet friend's family had been interned during World War II because they were Japanese. Had all their property been confiscated?

It was a time of change for me, as I transitioned from girl to woman, but the world around me was changing, too. My teachers filled my head with goals more lofty than becoming a wife and mother. The nuns, perhaps because they did not have husbands or children, were occupied with politics and what was going on in the world to an extent I'd never before witnessed. Although I had heard my parents discuss the news, they did so in such a way that made it seem inconsequential in our household.

To my mind, Sister Mary Damien was an expert on current affairs. With her holy habit skirt swirling around her ankles and her sprayed white coif stiffly structured about her face, she entered the classroom like a Staff Sergeant in charge.

"Take out your pens and paper and get ready to write your congressman," she ordered.

"Begin with the salutation: Dear Congressman, and spell his name properly. Did you hear me? Start writing!"

I sat stupefied. Congressman? I didn't know the names of my congressmen, or my senator, for that matter. Sister Damien would have none of this. She promptly marched us down to the Principal's office to teach us to use the congressional books there to find the names and addresses of our elected representatives. I barely remembered anything from the dull civics class I'd had before high school, but I never forgot this.

I was convinced that Sister Damien believed it was a venial sin not to know who your elected representatives were. It was without a doubt a mortal sin not to write your senator and congressmen regularly. I say congress*men*, as there were no congress*women* to be found in that era.

We spent several days working on our letters. Sister checked them for perfect penmanship, grammar, and the manner in which we expressed our individual points of view. We prepared satchels of letters in class and hand-carried an old, stained postage sack, rumored to have been stolen from the US Postal Service by our dear Sister, to the local post box. As we dragged the bag carrying the letters expressing views that had been carefully aligned with the "social justice" ethics of our activist teacher, her ideas resonated with me. Politics and the workings of the government came alive to me that year for the first time.

Sister Damien had never heard of "Liberation Theology," but her ideas were similar to those that later originated in South America in the movement led by traditional Catholics who were opposed to the Sandinista regime in Nicaragua. She would hardly have called herself a Marxist, but she was all for women's liberation as well as freedom for those oppressed.

However, she never verbally criticized the Church. It wasn't until 1971 that a Roman Catholic priest, Gustavo Gutierrez, wrote the seminal *Theology of Liberation* arguing that the gospels of Jesus were active and demanded that political and social action be taken on behalf of the poor and oppressed. The idea grew out of the Marxist-influenced analysis that attributed poverty to capitalist economic exploitation.

The liberation theologians reprimanded the Catholic Church for condoning the system instead of siding with the oppressed victims. According to Gutierrez, true liberation has three main dimensions: First, it involves political and social liberation—the elimination of the immediate causes of poverty and injustice. Second, liberation involves the emancipation of the poor, the marginalized, the downtrodden, and the oppressed from all "those things that limit their capacity to develop themselves freely and in dignity." Third, liberation theology involves liberation from selfishness and sin, a re-establishment of a relationship with God and with other people. When I became familiar with the movement in the 1970s, I realized that I had been introduced to these very ideas years earlier in high school.

Sister Damien read aloud every bit of the landmark decision US Supreme Court *Brown v. Board of Education of Topeka* 347 US 483 (1954) that had just come down, and declared that state laws establishing separate schools for black and white students denied black children equal education opportunities and were unconstitutional. She detailed the importance of the decision, explaining to us that these laws violated the 14th amendment. "Pay attention to what's going on in the South," she instructed.

Pay attention. The only thing I knew about the South was that it was full of cotton, rednecks, rich white folks in mansions like Tara in *Gone with the Wind,* poor black folks in shacks, and everyone spoke with a long Southern drawl. I wanted no part of it.

I'd had no clue what had been going on in the South until Sister Damien began to read the newspapers to us and follow the lawmakers in Washington daily. The South seemed worlds away from my life in the northwest. I suppose that Seattle was segregated, too, but living in an all-white neighborhood in suburbia, I'd never noticed it prior to high school, nor had I ever had a reason to go into black neighborhoods that were miles from my house yet in the heart of my high school community.

Sister Charles Marie, another one of our teachers, was an independent, no-nonsense woman who drilled into us the need to stand up for ourselves as women and empower our futures by defining our views concerning city, state and world events, and speaking out about them.

Although I'd never before known people of color in my school or neighborhood, now I had diverse classmates, and the ideas I heard echoed the sentiments of my parents, who, if only in theory, continually reminded me, "All men (and women) are created equal in the eyes of God, and don't you ever think otherwise! We're all God's children."

This was a simple statement of my father's enduring faith, and I believed it wholeheartedly. When political racism came home to roost, influenced by my inner-city friends, I, too, responded with horror upon hearing of Rosa Parks' arrest in Montgomery, Alabama, after the bus driver asked her to give up her seat to a white man and she refused. This event launched a bus boycott and the eventual desegregation of the bus system. It was the first time I ever heard the name of Martin Luther King, Jr., the young pastor who led the boycott.

Sister Damien raged on about social justice, and little by little, I understood the importance of our "voices being heard in Washington."

High school was crammed with new ideas and new experiences. I met teens from all over Seattle at the Knights of Columbus and CYO (Catholic Youth Organization) sponsored sock hops and parties. I discovered boys, and they discovered me. Home consisted of siblings laughter, chores and babies, housework and homework, never ending but none of it stopped me from having lots of new friends.

By the time I was sixteen, I had four younger sisters. Gloria, my youngest sister was born on December 18, 1955, and when my mother awoke the chapel bells in the hospital were playing "Gloria in Excelsios Deo," and so she named her sweet baby girl Gloria.

Sunday afternoon jam sessions were held downtown and my friends and I gathered to listen to the Rhythm and Blues of "Little Richard, singing *"Tuttti Frutti."*

We marshaled in the new sound with Bill Haley and the Comets performing, "Rock around the clock tonight. . ." or his "Shake Rattle and Roll," and "Crazy Man, Crazy Man."

It was the first time I had ever seen blacks dancing with whites together attending the same social functions. The musicians were all black.

The Twist was popular and I was crazy for dancing. We ushered in a new era of Rock and Roll. My soft pink angora sweater was my favorite, bought with money I had earned babysitting the neighbor's kids. I usually wore it with a black pencil skirt or a poodle skirt of felt with cutout icons of music notes, or poodle dogs which covered miles of crinoline slips.

My friend Vilma and I one night simply took off our crinoline underskirts and stuffed them into the trunk of the car in order to be able to fit the gang into the car to park along the road adjacent to the waters of Puget Sound near my home.

Glenn, my on and off boyfriend, kidded me.

"That's it; all you're taking off is your gargantuan underskirt?"

Friendships flourished in high school and I created bonds with not only Janet and Vilma, but also Gerri, Connie, Bobbi, Liz, Patti and Sandy.

I was in love with Glenn Darwin Smith and finally by the end of high school, he with me. We took long Sunday afternoon drives and made picnics to eat along the shores of Puget Sound. We watched "Rebel without a Cause," at the drive-in movies, double dating with Sandy and Richard, our friends. Glenn had a DA (ducktail) haircut accentuating his blond curls, and he rolled his short-sleeved T-shirt over a pack of cigarettes to hold them in place on his bicep just as Marlon Brando did in "On the Waterfront." He was a teen-age girl's dream.

I dated throughout high school and my studies were not my priority. The nuns, especially sister Charles Marie who nagged me relentlessly to improve my grades and use my God given talents, constantly reminded me of my lax study habits, but I got by. If my GPA plummeted, I studied and restored it, but it was easier to wing it.

I also dated Michael J. who drove a new red convertible and became the envy of the neighborhood when he picked me up for a date. My mother's friend, an older married woman, said to me, "He is the coolest cat I've ever seen. Don't let that one go."

Corky (James) Bader, another beau, spotted me in the rain in my yellow slicker at a high school football game and with my auburn red hair plastered to my face, he called out "red and yella, catch a fella and I'm the fella." We soon began dating and I remember dancing slow and close to Elvis singing "any way you want me."

The first time I saw Elvis was on the Ed Sullivan show where he sang, "Love me tender, love me true." Molly and I were astounded and talked long into the night in our bedroom about the sexy new idol. Molly claimed she was in instant love for life.

Glenn and I were doomed from the beginning and we never developed the relationship in the way we imagined until it was too late for us. He had agreed to take me to my Senior Prom, and I told him a week before the Prom that I was going to enter the Catholic convent in Oregon where I had been accepted for the late summer class. Glenn looked directly into my eyes.

"Susan, our prom date is off. You can stay home or get another date. Telling me at the last minute, what is wrong with you? We had so many plans.

"Plans," I said, "For what? I am only sixteen."

Devastated, not understanding what the prom had to do with me entering the convent, I pleaded with him. "Please Glenn, we will have so much fun, my mom made me a new dress. Why won't you go with me?"

"Susan you are crazy, man just crazy, the convent? What? You want to be a nun and never marry and have babies? This is news to me."

Sometimes in the years that followed, in moments of solitude, I swear I could hear him sing into my ear with his soft, melodious voice. "Wake up little Susie, wake up little Susie, we've both been asleep, wake up, the movie's over, it's four o'clock and we're in trouble deep. What're we gonna tell your mama, what're we gonna tell your pa?". . . Recorded by the Everly Brothers.

It took me a long time to realize that his sensitivity paralleled mine and that he was deeply hurt by my rejection. I stayed home from the prom and cried myself to sleep, missing Glenn and all my friends. I never wore the silky lavender dress my creative mom had so artfully designed for me.

My brother Robb grew well, graduated from high school, and left home to enter the Navy Submarine School back east. The summer I graduated from high school, he wrote to me from the Naval Command post in Yokosuka, Japan about love and Glenn and the convent, giving me his brotherly advice. In part, his letter read,

"I don't know what to say except that there's a lot of fish in the sea and a doll like you doesn't need a hook to catch them. Go out with different fellows and have some fun, but keep it clean. If you are still thinking of him (Glenn), then time will tell. As to the idea of the convent, that is a special life!

Love,

Robb

Robb married his high school sweetheart, Linda who he met in art class where he sat behind her. He was married to her the rest of his life.

I learned many new ideas in my high school years but most of all I think that my thinking was changed forever. It is said that an empath's way can be finely tuned from close contact with other empaths. I believe that several of the Holy Names Sisters taught me to be more empathetic to the less fortunate and they also cultivated within my soul a sense of social responsibility that took root in high school and never left me.

Chapter 3
1957, 1958 – Oswego, Oregon: Vocation

With graduation behind me, I entered the Holy Names convent on schedule in August as a postulant, a term used to define a candidate for the Sisterhood. Postulancy lasted for six months. After postulancy, we advanced to novice status. Novices studied further for one year without taking any vows to re-affirm their choice. The novice period allowed us to adjust to community life and to re-examine our religious commitment.

The convent was located on the grounds of Marylhurst College in Oswego, Oregon. It was a teaching order, and I chose it because of my desire to write and teach. Young as I was, I knew that my vocation was to fill a "call to service" and had no doubts about the life I had chosen. I was happy in the convent with its quiet halls filled with silent nuns rustling their homespun habits as they strode through the sanctuary tending to their daily assignments.

St. Teresa of Avila had been a mystic, and, feeling a kinship with her, I had taken her name as my confirmation name. For those who may not be familiar, confirmation is a Catholic sacrament given at the beginning of adolescence whereby one adds a saint's name to their given name. The idea is to strive to be like the holy saint. St. Teresa was a Carmelite nun, part of a contemplative order, and she wrote many books about her visions of Mary and Jesus. In this, I felt an affinity with her, due to my visions of Mary as a child. St. Teresa achieved the power to levitate through her devotion of "ecstasy or rapture" in prayer, which also fascinated me.

I loved the rituals of the Catholic faith and the discipline of the daily structure, but some things were difficult for me. In the past, my parents had always listened to me when I chose the courses I wanted to study. I hated math, but loved to read and write, and I adored foreign languages. They didn't force me to excel in what wasn't important to me because they understood that I knew my own mind. They helped me to achieve my goals. My mother always read and reviewed the stories I wrote and listened to and encouraged me at every step.

It was different in the convent. College courses in the convent were assigned by the Novice Mistress, who made the final decision on each postulant's curriculum. She was in charge of both postulants and novices, and—along with the college advisors—had the final say as to their academic and spiritual advancement while in the convent. I wanted to study Spanish, but they assigned me French. They also signed me up for archery when I wanted tennis. Archery turned out to be quite a challenge. I ended up loving it, but it was humiliating not to be able to choose my own classes. That was the point, I imagine—teaching me humility.

In a rebellious mood, my postulant friend, Joan, and I sat on the lawn under a shady oak tree outside the convent and complained about our inability to choose for ourselves, but we realized in the end we had it made.

"I love the Logic/Epistemology class we take together, don't you Joan?" I said.

"Yes, it's the best by far of them all," Joan agreed.

"Oh, Joan, I love Philosophy, too! I wish we could read the works of the philosophers all day long and then talk about them at dinner. Most days, we must be silent at mealtime. I miss talking at dinnertime since we always had discussions around the table in my family."

"And this idea of blind obedience already irritates me," I continued "Do you think it will get worse as we go along? I'm having a hard time with others doing all my thinking for me and choosing all my classes and my recreation, too."

Joan answered, "I guess I never really thought about it. The only vow I really did consider was Chastity because I believed that would be the hardest vow to keep: to give up men and love and sex, and of course, having babies. Of the three vows, we'll take at the First Vow Ceremony at the end of Canonical year: Poverty, Chastity and Obedience; perhaps Obedience will be just as difficult to keep as Chastity.

"Poverty doesn't seem to be an issue at this convent. In my house, my parents always worried about money and there was never enough. Here in the convent, no one ever talks about money. We drive custom-built Mercedes. We have lovely grounds beside the river; we eat well; our dental and doctor appointments are made for us, and we never see a bill; and though we'll be sewing our own clothes, including our habits, that's not so bad. At least I'll finally learn to sew properly. And, we have all the books we can read even if we're not allowed to read *Lady Chatterley's Lover*. I feel like I'm well off."

"I agree, the books are great here at the college library, and besides, Joan, I already read *Lady Chatterley's Lover* when I was sixteen. We certainly have most all the classics and a wide range of books written by many philosophers, not just the Catholic ones. I also like our studies of St. Thomas Aquinas—especially when we discuss his ability to apply rational analysis to theological questions. His synthesis of philosophy and revelation, as well as his five ways of understanding God are based on Aristotle's idea of the 'unmoved mover' or 'uncaused cause' and are the real things I want to discuss. I love the class!"

Later that day, we took the path along the Willamette River from Marylhurst College back to the Novitiate—the house where our religious order lived. We stopped to peer through the bushes at some boys who stood on the shore of the river with a boat and called to us to join them. One of them shouted, "Hey, who's there? Are you from the college? Want to come for a swim and a boat ride? Come out from behind those bushes so we can see you better!"

We had no bathing suits and we were dressed in our plain black postulant dresses and granny shoes. I poked just my head out to answer, "We're in a rush right now. We have an appointment. Can you guys meet us tomorrow, same time, after class, and we can swim then? We'll bring a picnic lunch."

A booming voice hollered back, "It's a date! There're three of us, and we'll be here tomorrow, same time. You ladies bring the food. We'll bring the beer."

We ran back to the convent and planned our interlude as if the unknown boys were our lovers. We saved rolls from our dinner, putting them in our pockets. I snuck into the pantry later that evening after study period to see what else I could find. Per the culinary directions of a willing nun just out of Canonical year, I stole some ham, bread, carrots, cookies and milk for our lunch. I couldn't find any sodas. We made up sandwiches, but I couldn't locate condiments in the large pantry and dared not take the risk to further search for them because just then two elderly nuns entered the pantry looking for some Irish tea, and I had to get out, fast. Thus, the sandwiches would have to be dry.

The next morning before dawn, we crept to the river's edge during Prayer and Meditation. We stashed the picnic and our regular swimsuits from home covered in the dishtowels we'd borrowed from the kitchen linens. We'd also brought bigger towels purloined from the laundry room for our swimming adventure.

Later, we walked anxiously from class down the narrow pathway through the high bushes of Oregon laurel to the exact place we'd hidden our lunch. Laughter issued from the boat moored at the riverside.

We took off our dresses, thigh-high black stockings, and our nun's shoes and put on our bathing suits, eager to meet the boys. We hid our clothes well in the underbrush so no one from the convent would happen upon them and start looking for us. Undaunted, we emerged and walked to the shore, picnic food in a kitchen towel and our communal white bath towels in our hands.

The boys appeared, and after a few introductions, helped us into the boat. Moving downstream, we anchored away from the college and ate our lunches. One of the boys complained about the dry sandwiches, but Joan quipped, "We're all out of mayo and mustard, students on a budget, you know."

"Have a beer, Susan! Milk's too tame for someone like you," a boy named Dan told me.

"Oh, I don't like beer, do you have any wine?" I replied airily.

"No," Dan joked, "We assumed all college girls liked beer, even the ones from Marylhurst."

Joan took a bottle of beer to be polite, and I watched her sip a bit then pour a little into the river when no one was looking. The other two boys, Tom and Philip, had a few beers before they swam with us in the river near the boat.

We had to be mindful so as not to miss Matins, our evening prayer time. We couldn't wear watches in the convent, so we asked the boys to remind us of our alleged "appointment." After our swim, we flirted and chatted awhile with the guys before we swam ashore.

"Nice to meet you all, goodbye and thanks for the boat ride!" We waved them off and hid in the brush, swiftly changing back into our postulants' dresses so we could scurry back to the Novitiate. Joan had the foolish idea to eat grass so that there'd be no smell of beer on her breath. She chomped down a handful while running through the brush.

"Well that was an interesting rendezvous," I commented. We broke into uncontrollable laughter that crippled our run all the rest of the way to our dormitory. When we were safe inside the hallway, I looked at Joan. Her teeth had turned green from the grass. I told her about it and we howled hysterically again.

Sister Petronella came around the corner and told us to silence ourselves. She said if she saw us talking or loitering again, she'd give us double housework.

"Let's tell Sister Caryl. She'll get such a kick out of our adventure," Joan suggested.

"No, no!" I shrieked. "We can't let anyone know! If we do, someone will tell the Novice Mistress—probably one of those goodie-two-shoes from our set—and we'll get booted out of here. Is that what you want?"

In retrospect, I think the boys must have known that we were from the convent all along, and they wanted to get a close-up glimpse of some nuns, particularly those that would hide their clothes and go for a swim. Our hair was quite short; we wore no other clothes but our swimsuits—no cover-ups or shorts and shirts over the suits—and we carried only large white towels with us, not beach towels. We had garnered some lipstick from a slightly older nun who had already taken her first vows by telling her it was for a project at school. She loaned us a bright red tube. Why she owned a lipstick in the first place, we could only guess. We had no purses, no shoes. Maybe it had been obvious to the boys that we were from the Novitiate, and they were curious about us convent escapees. At that point in my life, I was pretty much your normal, sometimes-rebellious teenager, with no clue of what was to come.

The routine and discipline of convent life continued, and I settled back down into my studies, at least until one night in early spring. That night, I went into the dorm where my single bed was located in a small alcove partitioned off by a curtain, crawled under the covers, and fell into a deep sleep. At 3:10 a.m., I suddenly awoke, feeling that someone was in the room. I know what time it was because I jerked upright, and I could see the illuminated clock on the wall.

The vision of my mother hovered above the end of my bed. There were tears in her eyes. She spoke softly and said, "Susan, please come home now. I need you." She wore a soft nightgown of pale blue.

When I tried to answer her, she was gone.

The following morning, disturbed by the vision I'd had of my mother, I waited in line outside the door of my Novice Mistress to talk with her about it, though I didn't know exactly what I would say. When my turn came, I entered her office and blurted out what I'd seen, calling it a "dream". "Sister, may I please call my parents?" I asked anxiously. "Something's wrong; my mother is asking for me."

As postulants, we weren't normally allowed to communicate with the outside world during the season of Lent. The Novice Mistress read and held our letters until Easter. We were then allowed to read them on the religious holiday. The Mistress rose from her desk without a word, went to a file cabinet beside her desk and handed me a letter from my father.

Daddy wrote:

April 1, 1958

Dear Sue,

> *We have great news to tell you! Your mother is pregnant, and this time, I am sure it will be a second boy after five girls. I'm happy we'll have another baby in the house. Coming home from work to the family and a smiling baby always makes me happy. We will not be coming to visit you in Portland at Easter since Mother is ill with morning sickness, and we cannot have her vomiting the entire trip.*

Daddy's letter continued with banter about my siblings. He also mentioned how much he missed riding the bus into Seattle with me in the mornings.

Enclosed with his letter was a note from my mother:

Dear Susan,

I am fine and the morning sickness will stop soon; it always does. Daddy thinks it's a boy for sure this time, but we will see. I think he might be right. All is well with me, but I have some rather sad news about your friend, Corky Bader. Dearest Susan, he was killed in an auto accident last week. Did you know that he had stopped by the convent and tried to visit with you on his way back from Mexico with a friend? The Novice Mistress wouldn't let him into the convent even though he fibbed and told her he was your cousin, so I doubt she did tell you of his attempt to visit.

Molly and I went to the Funeral and the Rosary; it was quite a sad event. Corky was so young, handsome, and full of life. I will pray for his soul. His parents are devastated, as you can imagine. I have enclosed the Baders' address, as I know you will want to write to them. Corky was a special boy, and I know he is with God in heaven now.

Gloria is such a cute toddler—smiling and happy all the time. I love looking at her sweet face. We all send our prayers.

Love,

Mother

Corky had been number one on Mom's list of suitors for me before I entered the convent. He was adorable, Catholic, from a good family, smart, witty and wonderful to be around. According to my mother, he was perfect marriage material.

Glenn Smith—with whom I was smitten—on the other hand, was at the bottom of my mother's hierarchy of marriageable men. Glenn pined for me while I was in the convent and hung around my house so much, he soon became my mother's project. She invited him to visit and showered him with her prayers and religious platitudes. He studied Catholicism under her tutelage and was baptized in the faith while I was away. No one mentioned this to me until after I returned home. Looking back, I wonder why my Mother never wrote that she had converted Glenn. It wasn't like her to play missionary; she was much too busy with her family. I think she was hedging her bets in case I left the convent (with or without finishing college) to marry him.

I couldn't focus on my college curriculum or postulancy duties after having my vision and reading those letters. I worried that Mother was about to give birth to her seventh child and needed me. I also grieved the loss of my friend, Corky.

Corky's death made me think about how I'd have felt if it had been one of my parents' death, or a sibling's, and I wasn't allowed to leave the convent for their funeral. I wanted to be with Corky's family and could not. I wrote his parents a long letter and wept into the night after I mailed it.

I missed Seattle, my family, and friends. The realization that my life would be so very different as a Sister made me re-think my intentions. Did I really want to stay in the convent? I began to feel that it wasn't a good fit for me, after all. Easter came and went; then summer; then Ceremony time—when I readied myself for the canonical year spent in preparation for my first vows of poverty, chastity and obedience. I doubted the strength of my commitment.

I resolved to leave the convent for good shortly thereafter, abandoning my dream of becoming Sister Maura Rose, the Noviate name I had chosen for myself. The vision

I'd had of my mother calling me home made me realize that it was not yet time to leave my family.

The only person I told of my decision besides my Novice Mistress was my assigned convent Angel. Each postulant was assigned a novice to help her to adjust to convent life and my cousin, Sister Caryl, was mine. I missed her dearly when I left. I did go back to watch her take her final Vows as Sister Mary Carolyn Frances at her Ceremony in August.

She wrote soon afterwards:

August 8, 1958

Dear Susan,

> *Thank you so much for the beautiful roses and book,* The Living Bread. *It is very nice of you to remember me so generously. I was glad you came to my ceremony, and it was so much fun to see our Dolan cousins, Honora, and Kathleen, too.*

Much of the body of the letter after that was filled with remembrances and personal references to our parents and siblings and convent life. Then she continued:

> *Well dear cousin "Angel," be good and have lots of fun. Don't work too hard, and don't forget you're always in my prayers. I pray that you are happy in whatever you choose to do. Remember all my "speeches" reminding you that "you are a wonderful person." I love you and will always treasure our good times. (Thank the Lord the bad ones weren't any worse!)*

> *You looked so darling at the Ceremony. I like your taste.*

The flowers on the altar were beautiful, and the book is very good. I don't want to quit writing but it looks like I'm at the end of the page.
Lovingly in Jesus and Mary,
Sister Mary Carolyn Frances

There were two huge lessons I learned while in the convent that I have never forgotten. One was that my mom had given up more of herself and her former life to be a mother and wife than those living amongst the convent walls had. The life of a nun was full of sacrifice; I understood that. I admired Sisters who had let go of much yet still seemed genuinely happy in spirit. Sister Petronella and Sister Miriam Elizabeth were two such idols. My dear Caryl and my cousins, Honora and Anne, who were Dominican nuns, seemed satisfied, as well. But the desire and competition for honors and accolades amongst some of the Sisters was something I'd never seen in my mother. When I compared some of the women in the convent to my mother, it seemed to me that my mother's sacrifices for her family far outweighed the nuns' sacrifices.

The second thing I learned in depth in the convent was the art of meditation and prayer. Daily (when I was supposed to be praying), I trained my eyes on several of the older nuns who seemed to transcend the cold, the dark, and their hunger, so that they almost appeared to levitate before us at the altar. Young as we were, we all knew this was not ordinary prayer. It was some type of ability to focus their minds and bodies in order to alter their states of consciousness.

I began to believe that there were two types of meditation, the mystical and the secular. I was aiming for the mystical, but never quite seemed to attain the goal. I was slowly learning the secular form, but some of these nuns had gone beyond it into the art of the mystic. I don't think any of them would have said that was so, but in my soul I knew it to be true.

We rose early, awakening to the bell that rang like a siren through the dorm, and went to chapel long before Mass began. We knelt or stood with our arms upraised in prayer and/or meditation for over an hour before the start of Mass. No one had told us to do this, but we copied the older Sisters and the ones we admired.

At first, I thought I was just generally praying for myself, my family back home, and the ability to reach my goals, but before long, I began to focus more on contemplation, the practice of thinking about meaning—such as the meaning of prayer. I focused on concepts and questions such as, "How is prayer different from meditation?"

Sisters Amy and Joan were my best friends. We attempted to monitor our breathing to determine whether we were just praying or were actually in some meditative, dream, or sleep state. We began to notice that the pain due to uplifting our arms for extended periods of time seemed to dissipate the deeper into our consciousness we went. Joan was excited. "We've crossed a threshold somehow. There's no more pain! Is it mind over matter, or are we numb? Truly, I have no pain at all."

She confided to us that she mostly prayed when she needed things from God. "I pray because I need God to help me get through this postulancy and upcoming Canonical year before I take vows. Meditating seems different. It seems to me that prayer often turns into meditation but meditation can't turn into prayer. Sometimes I keep repeating, 'God, help, God help me,' over and over again."

Amy replied, "I'm always praying for guidance, even if it's to find the glasses I just took off. I pray we have dessert with dinner tonight—hopefully, something chocolate. Watch Sister Owen and Sister Thomas tomorrow morning. They must be meditating, not praying, because they're so far beyond our capabilities with this spiritual thing. Watch their breath. I can hardly take my eyes off them in the chapel—which doesn't help my own spiritual focus."

"Amy, I know what you mean about meditation—those nuns are unearthly to watch. I have a strong faith in God, but I can't quite understand this art of prayer and meditation. I'm thinking that prayer is in fact the opposite of meditation; it's non-thinking. In prayer, I seek answers from God by getting rid of all outside distractions so that I can focus my thoughts on the prayer itself and my communication with God. I am speaking to God in my prayers, telling him my fears and hopes. That's prayer."

I turned to Joan and continued, "Joan, don't you think your phrase of 'God help me,' repeated over and over again becomes a mantra, so maybe you're meditating and not realizing it?"

Meditation, I concluded, was in essence a quieting of the mind so that God could speak to me, and that idea set me on fire. "Is God talking to me?" I wondered.

When I tried to clear my mind—by following my breath as it came in through my nostrils, then down into my lungs, then back up and out of my lungs, and back through the cycle again, while focusing on a particular candle on the altar—my body did indeed seem to change. I could only accomplish this "letting go" of my thoughts for a few seconds or a minute at first. I would get distracted or sneak a peek at Amy or Joan to see if they were watching Sister Owen or Sister Thomas in the chapel. However, over time I was slowly able to quiet my mind to nothingness.

I discovered a practice that combined both prayer and meditation. I sat quietly, and instead of attempting to clear my mind, I would pray to God and witness that prayer without judgment or comparisons to other forms of silence. I would pray for myself, my family, for my sisters in the convent and for everyone in the world. By witnessing as I prayed for others in this way, it seemed to combine both prayer and meditation. I would be mindful of either an imaginary image or real image in the chapel. Sometimes, I used a particular part of the church's architecture, or I'd pick one single flower or leaf from an altar plant and concentrate on it to create a receptive awareness of the plant until I felt I was one with it.

I tried this technique while eating a cookie for dessert one night after dinner. Since we couldn't talk, I entertained myself by focusing my attention solely on the peanut butter cookie itself until I became one with the cookie. It seemed to work to enhance the flavor of the peanut butter. However, I kept this idea to myself, not sure if Amy or Joan would appreciate the mindful meditation of a cookie.

Now, I realize that such meditation is the very essence of my life's work as a psychic. I learned to meditate in the convent and have never stopped. Meditation is primary to my psychic practice. My "readings" are done in a "trancelike" state. I must go into a deep meditative state in order to tune out all noise except what is in my head and what my client is saying to me. I meditate every day of my life. I still feel that the convent was an integral part of my spiritual journey, even though I made the deliberate choice to leave it.

Chapter 4
1958 – Seattle, Washington: Moving On

I returned home from the convent to Seattle in time for my brother's birth. Little Eddie was born that September, and my dad was ecstatic to have another son after five girls. Edward Joseph was the last of my parents' seven children. Expertly, I changed diapers and did laundry. I cooked family-style stews, chicken cacciatore, and my mother's favorite: fresh fish that Daddy bought directly from Seattle's fishermen.

I ironed uniforms for my sisters and helped my mother with the new baby. I lived at home for about a year and began working at the Canadian Bank of Commerce as a teller in downtown Seattle. The daily exchange with the customers was uplifting to me and I made new friends, different from my peers, older than me. Phyllis and Dixie had both been married and divorced, and Joan, a single friend, was several years older than I.

I was ready to embrace my banking career, so I took a series of banking courses through the American Bankers Association and studied hard to pass at the top of the class. My parents had expected me to go to Seattle University, the Catholic college, when I got back home, but I wanted to get a job. The convent had changed me from a girl to a woman, and I didn't fit in at home anymore. I loved my siblings, but I was eager to discover the world.

My mother needed me less as the baby grew, and I felt it was time I moved into an apartment downtown, complete with a roommate. I bought a contemporary white leather couch—a statement of freedom: no babies, no dog and no siblings to sit on it and muck it up. It was glorious.

I bought pots and pans from a door-to-door salesman, and cooked all the things I wanted but couldn't always have at home for dinner: halibut cheeks, Alaskan king crab and salmon straight from the fishing boats at Seattle's Pier. I learned to make spaghetti and meatballs, and ate it with crusty sourdough French bread. I mastered the Caesar salad. When I left something in the refrigerator, it was actually still there when I returned home; if I saved a brownie for later, I ate it later.

My roommate was a friend who had also left the convent, and she never filched my sweaters. They were always in the same place I left them. If she even borrowed so much as a bobby pin, she called out to me, "Can I borrow your hair clip? I'll return it in the morning." The next morning, she did as she promised. Such was the luxury of my new life without four sisters.

I discovered Chinese takeout, and eating it while listening to Jazz became a staple. The first LP I bought for myself was Dave Brubeck's album, "Time Out," and I also purchased a record player of my own. *Seeds of Contemplation* by Thomas Merton, a Trappist monk whose writings fed my soul, was the first book I bought with my own money.

I was introduced to Bill, a Greek man a few years older than I, with whom I fell in love. In due time, he asked me to marry him, presenting me with a lovely diamond ring. It all seemed perfect until he took me home to meet his mother. She looked me over critically during our first meeting. She served me a plate of sugar cookies slivered with almonds that smelled of cinnamon along with a glass of Ouzo and said to her son in Greek, "She is lovely, but much too young to be your wife."

He later told me that in order to sanction the marriage, she had one condition: I was to go to Greece for a year to learn the language and the customs. I was also to be schooled in the culinary art of preparing Greek food. I was to stay with her family in Greece, and if we still wanted to marry after that year, she would approve the marriage. Bill assumed my acquiescence was a done deal.

Though Seattle's Greek community embraced me as Bill's fiancé, and I loved them as my own (and my love affair with Greece has never left me), a year away from home was too long for me. I also felt Bill was destined to kowtow to his mother always. That scared me. I panicked at the thought of being in a foreign country and at being controlled by his relatives for a whole year. Then, I didn't believe I could handle it, but how I have changed! Today, I would run to Greece just for the opportunity.

I broke off our engagement. Bill refused to take the ring back, thinking it would all work out. I mailed him his ring. (In those days, one trusted the U.S. Post Office.) I refused to take his phone calls.

Finally, I realized that I had been hasty and unwilling to listen to his side of the story. We agreed to meet. He told me he had promised his father on his deathbed that he would only marry a woman his mother favored. He also thought that the year wait was reasonable and the least he could do to please his mother. I knew his mother was certain we would soon forget one another.

"Bill, I can't go to Greece. I would be too lonely not to see you or my family. I think I'd miss everyone too much, including you. It doesn't seem fair to have to go live halfway across the world in order to marry someone here in Seattle."

"Susan, if I could go with you I would, but I have to work. I can't be gone from my job for a year. I'll come see you at Christmastime."

He just didn't seem to realize that he was asking too much of me, so I moved on.

The convent was behind me, but my spiritual seeking had only just begun. I had been intrigued by the introduction to meditation I'd gotten in the convent setting, but soon became seduced by Eastern religions and the art of meditation and traditions in varied cultures. Although meditation is universally practiced, it is certainly more formalized in the East as a spiritual discipline. This is especially true in yoga as it attempts to transform consciousness through mental control, to teach its students to transcend beyond the absence of thought.

I began what I had started in the convent, to concentrate on a single object like the flame of a candle for breath control, but before long, I began to sit in the Lotus position and use a mantra. I studied Buddhism and its detached awareness but also incorporated aspects of Zen, the best-known method of meditation in the West.

I was captivated by the Eastern religions, but the Catholic mystics still held my interest, and I read further into their meditative writings. St. John of the Cross and St. Francis of Assisi had experienced many apparitions and/or experiences of interior locution—that's what the Catholic Church calls auditory or telepathic ideas or messages that occur without visions.

I was learning the art of banking as a teller and lessons in life that were completely apart from the ones I'd learned in the convent from Dixie, my boss, whom I adored. She was smart, ambitious, beautiful, and dated a hockey player on Seattle's team, the Totems. She was divorced, the first single mother I had ever met.

She took me under her wing and began to mentor me. I remember the first time she took me to the main post office downtown and showed me how the bank sent Canadian money back to Canada. We carried large litigation-type briefcases out to the curb in front of the bank. A cab had been called, and we filed into the back seat settling in for the short ride. With the black cases between us, she instructed the driver where to go and to wait for us once we got there.

As we bundled our coats around us, she touched my hand and motioned for me to look into her expensive purse that gaped partially open where she had unzipped the leather. I peered inside, and, to my utter amazement, I saw a shiny gun stuck in the inside pocket. My eyes widened, so she put a finger to her lips to signify that I shouldn't say anything. My heart beat violently, and I wasn't sure what to expect next. Up until that moment, I had only seen large hunting rifles, never a handgun or pistol.

Completely unglued, I monitored Dixie's every move until the cab stopped. We lugged the cases up the steps and the guard ushered us toward a private window at the end of the room in the post office marked, "Canadian Only."

Dixie undid the combination locks on the briefcases and proceeded to count out thousands and thousands of Canadian dollars to the man behind the window. After each stack was counted, the man put a red seal of wax embellished with the bank's emblem on the paper band that held the money together. This process was taking quite a long time, so another man came to help count and seal the money and place it into stacks ready to be sent to our head office in Canada. The money was sacked in burlap and fitted into wooden crates as soon as each bundle was finished. There were cracks in the crate, and I thought I could see money through the fissures in the wood.

Finished with our business, we found our waiting cab, and Dixie informed me that, from now on, I would be in charge of returning the Canadian money to the head office and that she would supervise.

"Dixie, I don't know if I can do this," I told her, knowing I'd have to carry a gun in my purse, too.

It was as if she'd read my mind when she said, "You will definitely need to learn how to handle a gun."

David, Vice President at the bank, and Dixie, took me out for target practice, and I learned to shoot quite well. The trips to the post office with the case of money and a gun in my purse soon became commonplace. I felt important and grown up.

I was introduced to a world of single and divorced people, with and without children, who had much more fun than my parents had ever imagined.

Joan was one of them, and she became my good friend, partly because we were close in age. She invited me to drive to California for a vacation with her and share expenses. I went along with the notion that if I got a job, I'd quit my bank job in Seattle and stay there. My mother encouraged me to go, so long as I promised to visit her sister and my beloved cousin, Honora, who both lived in the Berkeley Hills. Baby Eddie was older now, and I had helped her enough. She knew that I was ready to move on.

California opened me up to new ideas, new friends, and love. Later, being there led to a world of esoteric experiences in the realm of the metaphysical. But, I had much to learn before I would be ready to engage the spirit world. The Catholic teachings I had absorbed in my childhood prepared me for interaction with the Spirits. This other world wasn't foreign to me because I realized that some of the rites I had seen in church were linked to controlling it. The burning of incense, for instance, was done to keep the spirits in abeyance. Song also entranced the community of followers into a meditative state (as does chanting when seeking the condition that facilitates entrance into the spirit world). Many practices that I had assumed to be Christian or Catholic I later learned had been taken from ancient rituals associated with pagan and other beliefs. In retrospect, I realize that I never thought about what I knew or didn't know at this stage of my life; I simply believed I had a guardian angel, a protectorate that assisted me and helped me to know what or what not to do.

I don't actually recall having visions during this time, but I did have what I thought was an inner voice that always seemed to have my best interests at heart. It was more a knowingness of what was to come and where I would be led—like knowing without hesitation that I was to move to California and that I would never again live in Seattle.

It was Glenn, my high school boyfriend—not Bill, my Greek fiancé—who followed me to California.

Chapter 5
1959 – Oakland, California: Another World

"You have the job if you want it," the bank manager at the National Bank of Commerce in Oakland told me at the end of my second interview. "I'll review your references, and you can start next Monday if everything checks out."

My decision to stay in California was now supported by the reality of a new job.

I didn't send for my winter clothes from Seattle. New to the world of work in Oakland, I possessed few appropriate clothes, so I bought new ones in bright colors. A Californian wears colorful clothes in the daytime, but a San Franciscan wore black. I also bought a black sheath dress, and the black pencil skirts that were popular at the time.

I shared an apartment with an older woman named Edie from the bank until I could afford my own place. She was wonderful to me, and I became the daughter she never had. She was an interesting character, and she must have been a beauty in her day. Allegedly, she had been a prostitute or call girl of some sort before she "retired" and became a banker. I didn't care about that. She looked after me and gave me good advice. I loved her.

The three things I remember most about moving from the Pacific Northwest to California's Bay Area are: one, the incredible feeling of sunshine on my face almost every day; two, the energy of being alive; and three, the friendliness of the people I met. We spoke to one another on the street and engaged in conversations on a whim. It was a feeling that a new day was about to dawn, that something big was about to happen that would change and affect everyone. This feeling of expectancy permeated the streets of San Francisco and the entire Bay Area.

Exploring the Bay Area on weekends without a car took me to places I would never have been able to access had I not been on foot. I fell in love with the Italian community of North Beach. I could often be found walking through North Beach headed towards Broadway and the Parisian sidewalk café, Enrico's, where I sat drinking coffee and reading Kerouac's *On the Road*. Just being there made me long to go to Paris. I imagined its streets lined with wonderful sidewalk cafés where everyone spoke a different language but somehow exchanged ideas, and sat for hours drinking Dubonnet and *café au lait*.

Lenny Bruce and Faye Dunaway came into Enrico's one late afternoon, and I was starstruck. Kerouac frequented the place and I wanted to meet him after several sightings. I think he usually slept all day since he was more often spotted there in the wee hours of the morning when I had to sleep. At last, the day came! I lucked out when one of his friends invited me to come and sit with his crowd! I was too awestruck to say anything apart from the usual pleasantries. All I remember was that the conversation wasn't philosophical but dwelt instead on food—burgers to be exact. This was not what I had imagined. Kerouac soon drew a crowd to his table, and I exchanged no words of substance with him.

I made new friends just as the Beat Generation became a force in San Francisco. Writers like Jack Kerouac had moved there from New York. Jack claimed that prior to 1948, he and John Clellon Holmes had been discussing the meaning of the "lost generation" of the 1920s and the subsequent rise of Existentialism. Kerouac said, "This really is a 'beat generation'," and Holmes replied, "That's it; that's right, the 'Beat Generation'."

Kerouac considered himself a spokesperson for the beat generation. He wrote in *Lamb, No Lion* in 1958 that by the term "Beat," he didn't mean "tired or bushed, so much as it means *beato*, the Italian for beatific, to be in the state of beatitude like St. Francis, trying to love all of life, trying to be utterly sincere with everyone, practicing, kindness, cultivating joy of heart." He claimed that this could be done in our mad, modern world of multiplicities and millions by practicing a little solitude, going off by oneself occasionally to store up that most precious of gold: "the vibrations of sincerity."

I took his words as gospel.

Allen Ginsberg and John Clellon Holmes—and Sartre and Genet in France—were all writing (according to Kerouac) "like an inspired fever free of Bourgeois-Bohemian materialism."

I identified with Kerouac because he was brought up Catholic, was a French Canadian (my mother was Canadian, though not French), and he was an adventuresome spiritual seeker, like myself. I was fascinated by the idea of Existentialism. The atheistic individualistic version with which the term has become synonymous gave me fodder for thought.

City Lights Bookstore was a remarkable place. I took the bus across the Bay Bridge to the place where the bookstore still stands today on Columbus St. and browsed books by him and other writers of my time, buying one when I could afford it. I was drawn to the beauty of Eastern religions, especially Buddhism. Alan Watts—former Anglican priest and a leading American authority on Buddhism—criticized Kerouac's work as being "too subjective" regarding Buddhism. I thought this was crazy. Isn't all personal thought subjective?

The beat generation of the 1950s morphed before my eyes into the hippie counter-culture of the 1960s. Looking back, the difference between the two now seems to me to be that the intellectualism and spiritual quests of the beat generation grew more hedonistic as the hippie "flower children" of my beloved San Francisco moved in. People came from all over the US, even from the Midwest and the north. It seemed that everyone I met was revolting against their parents and society. They found their spiritual opening through drugs, distrusted the government, and protested the war in Vietnam. Some left for Canada rather than fight.

In the early days, politics and the Vietnam War permeated hippie idealism. However, this idealism seemed to fade until the movement became self-indulgent. Hippies engaged in promiscuous sex (AIDS was not known as a concern back then), drugs and rock and roll.

Many women my age came to San Francisco and became intoxicated by drugs and free love. They put their "love children" up for adoption in California in the early and mid-sixties. The state ran a database so that siblings and half-siblings could be adopted by the same parties. Many of these mothers returned to the civilized lives they had forsaken when disenchantment set in or they got tired of living on the streets.

During this time, I became a fan of Simone de Beauvoir because of her deep commitment to freedom and the emerging roles of women. Although she was an atheist (something, I knew I was not, nor would I ever be), I loved her work. "The Second Sex" in particular was a milestone in my journey to progressive thinking.

At night, the bank crowd went out together to listen to jazz at the Blackhawk in the Tenderloin, and my favorite performance of all time was when Amed Jamal played, "But not For Me" on the piano, my favorite instrument.

I hung out at the *Hungry I* (for intellectual) where no one ever asked me, "Are you twenty-one? Can I see your ID?" No one cared in those days; if you looked good, you got in to the club. I assumed the police looked the other way. (I was offered—and turned down—a job at the "Purple Onion" when I was nineteen and the drinking age was twenty-one. No one bothered to check my ID even then.)

I met a man at the *Hungry I* who was West Indian. He had caramel-colored skin and was quite handsome. He asked for my phone number, and soon we were dating. He took me dancing every weekend at the clubs. We checked in with one another during the week, and sometimes he came by after work and we went to dinner. I was happy with his company and eagerly looked forward to the times we could be together.

One day, after we'd been seeing each other for almost a year, I walked up the street to the drugstore to buy a few items during an afternoon break. I went down an aisle of the store, and there was my boyfriend accompanied by a West Indian woman holding a tiny baby. He nodded, and I stopped and stared at them in shock.

All I could think of to say was, "Hi, what are you doing here?"

He calmly introduced me as a colleague from work to the woman I assumed was his wife. I bit my tongue and left, mumbling, "Nice to see you."

When he came by my apartment that night, he couldn't understand what he had done wrong.

"Why didn't you tell me that you were married? That's what you did wrong!" I exclaimed.

"I'm not married, but it is my baby. Honestly, I didn't know about the baby. She was in the Caribbean and did not tell me about the baby until she came to visit."

He wanted to continue the relationship, but I was done. We never saw each other after that. I scoured my brain to examine why it never occurred to me that he might be married or with someone else. I'd been to his apartment many times, and there was never any evidence of a woman or a family. He was as single a man as I had ever seen, or so I thought. I had much to learn about men.

I had moved out from Edie's and was living in an apartment with another roommate. One evening the doorbell rang, and when I opened it, there before me stood Glenn Smith, suitcase in hand. He had come to renew our high school relationship, collect me, and take me back to Seattle to marry me. Unfortunately, all my romantic feelings for him were gone, and he no longer held any attraction for me. He slept on the couch that night and left the next day after a doleful farewell. I closed the chapter on my first love and let him go. I never saw him again.

Then several years ago one night in late fall, dreamlike he came to me, and I knew that he had crossed over to the other side. I mentioned to my sister that he had come to tell me he would see me again. A week or so later, my dear friend Connie from high school, who had been witness to my "love crazy" overtures towards Glenn, sent me his obituary cut from the *Seattle Times*. I noted that he had in fact died the same day he journeyed to my bedside. I thought, "Glenn, Godspeed. I have never forgotten how I felt about you, my first love."

I loved my job as a bank teller, and I enjoyed meeting all the customers, but one afternoon at 5:00 p.m., in marched the bank auditors, not something any of us enjoyed. A young Englishman, a new auditor for the bank, came over to my teller's cage and began to count the money in my bank drawer. When it all added up correctly, he moved on. The teller crew had to stay until every one of the tellers' drawers had been counted. As I got ready to leave, the auditor with the English accent came up to me and began to engage me in conversation.

I told him, "It's late, and I need to go home. Usually the auditors take us to dinner on the first day of the audit, and we explain all the procedures unique to this particular bank. I haven't eaten, and I need to get home." I wasn't looking for an invitation from him, just reciting the facts.

"When I want to invite a lady out to dinner, I will ask her," he said stiffly.

With his words ringing in my ears and embarrassment stinging my face, I left the bank and walked to the lakeside apartment I had recently rented on my own.

Several days later the auditor, Derek, the man who was later to become my husband, called and invited me to dinner. He had come to America from London, England, in the same era as the Beatles, sans guitar.

He asked me to marry him the week after we started dating and wanted it to be right away. When I called my parents to tell them I was getting married, they thought I was pregnant because of the rush, but I wasn't. I told my mom I wasn't and not to worry, that I had almost instantly known I was going to marry Derek, and evidently, he had too, since he'd asked me so quickly.

I called Father Erny, my parish priest from grammar school, and set the wedding date. "Father, please make sure that my mom understands I'm not pregnant. I don't want her to worry. She has enough already to worry about. I told her that I wasn't with child, but it wouldn't hurt if you mentioned it, too. She knows I wouldn't lie to you."

We married in Seattle a month after we met in my home parish with my family around me. My sister Gloria was three years old then and was my flower girl.

Chapter 6
1960s – Marriage and Motherhood

The thing that confounded me most during my first year of marriage wasn't the adjustment of learning to live with someone else—I had been raised in a houseful of people and had roomed with more since I'd left home. Rather, it was getting used to the fact that my husband couldn't sense what other people's behavior meant as I could. He couldn't tell what was about to happen in our lives, let alone in the lives of those closest to him. I realized then that my empathic ability to tune into others was an advantage and not the curse I had previously thought it to be.

Before I married, I kept most psychic things to myself, but I now realized that my mother and my sisters always seemed to know things about people and events before they happened, yet when I tried to talk to my husband in the same way I did with them, he couldn't comprehend what I was talking about.

Years later, I had a conversation with my sister Molly (now known by the spiritual name of Ananfaye) who is also psychic. She remembers thinking she must have been dumb because she knew things that others didn't. Dumb? I never thought I was dumb, not for a moment. I had little time during the years ahead, filled as they were with mothering young children, to wonder why I often knew things about people before they did, but I'd always been smart in school and chalked my knowing up to the fact that I was "smart." Unlike my sister, I thought my abilities had something to do with my intelligence.

At a bank party one evening, I casually remarked to my husband—referring to his boss, the president of the bank—"Gene's having an affair with his secretary, Laila, and he loves her. He doesn't want to be with his wife."

My husband laughed at what he referred to as my "overactive imagination."

I repeated this information each time it came to me whenever I was around his boss. Almost ten years later, the bank president built a beautiful new house for his wife and growing family.

My husband announced, "You were so wrong about Gene! He's such a great family man that he's built a beautiful new home for them all."

I said nothing. I knew my intuition was correct. Several months later, after his family had moved into the new house, he sold the old one, divorced his wife of ten years and married his secretary. Everyone at the bank was in an uproar at this news, but it was yesterday's paper to me. The realization that my sisters, my mother, and I all had what the Irish call the "second sight" was thrust upon me more strongly than ever before.

Derek and I wanted a baby, and our first child came to us swiftly and quietly, like a gift delivered unexpectedly. Motherhood now became the focus of my life. My wanderlust and desire to further my psychic development took second place to being a mother. We named our firstborn son Barry because we wanted a name that wasn't a family name. However, we found out later that my paternal great grandfather's given name was Greenberry, and his nickname was Berry, something I must have intuited at some level.

From the beginning, the bond between my son and me was so powerful I believed he had called out "Mama" to me from the spirit realm long before I ever cradled him in my arms. He was so affectionate, kissing and hugging me whenever he got a chance to cuddle. When he called me "Mama" and climbed into my lap for a story, my heart filled to overflowing. To this day, I "hear" him speak to me and stop to listen. When we later connect on this physical plane, he always says he was just speaking or thinking of me. I can sense when he's sad or in pain, and know at times he's with me in spirit, too, even when physically far away.

Barry had brown eyes and in the summer his skin would tan to a golden brown. He always had a smile for everyone and seemed delighted to be alive. He was the most adorable, cuddly baby, and, as he grew, he was the happiest little boy I'd ever seen, curious and always on the move. He could take anything apart and was never idle. He loved his Tonka trucks and cars, and played for hours in the dirt with them.

My children were the joys of my life, then and now.

The intervening years between the birth of my son and daughter, my world and the world of many Americans changed forever. At the time, being a mother and watching my children thrive filled me with joy. The world was changing rapidly and the politics of transformation unlocked more freedoms for many but not without cost.

On November 22, 1963, when my little son was a toddler, the first president I had been old enough to vote for was assassinated and the world as I had known it was gone forever. As many Americans did, I adored Jackie and followed the first family with little John, John and Caroline. For me President Kennedy inspired hope for America.

I remember the day well. I was working as a service Representative for the telephone company in their downtown Oakland office. Word came through the office that the president had been shot in Dallas, Texas. We tried to bring in televisions sets and watch the news but in the end they closed the office and we all went home in shock. It was agonizing to watch the drama. The streets were filled with people openly crying as they went about their daily tasks.

The murder of our president and the subsequent murder of his assailant, Lee Harvey Oswald by Jack Ruby remains an unknown even to this day. Most people I know think that there was more to it than a lone gunman. The Warren Commission investigated the murder and found there was no conspiracy but many people (including me) have their doubts to this day.

The incident shattered the illusion that we lived in a safe world and did little to prepare us for what was to come. It was the coming of age for television as the assassinations' and murders were witnessed "live" in our own homes. I watched my son more closely to keep him from harm's way and soon I was preparing for the birth of our daughter.

I was joyous when our tiny daughter arrived. She was a beautiful little girl, psychic from the moment she was born. Though premature and sickly, contracting pneumonia repeatedly, she was perfect. Sometimes, I believed her to be not human but from some angelic realm. I carried her around in my arms like one of the dolls I'd played with in my childhood. We named her Sheila, after Sister Sheila Ranger, SNJM—my beloved teacher when I was a sophomore in high school.

Sheila's pale blue eyes were the color of the summer sky, and with her dark black hair, she was indeed what the Irish call "Black Irish." (Black Irish carry the genes of the Moors who invaded Ireland long ago and mixed their blood with that of the Celts). I cut her hair into a "pixie", and it framed her sweet face in curly wisps resembling a halo.

Once an acquaintance said to me, "Your daughter has a very beautiful face, but I'm not so sure it's the face of a child." I was quite hurt by this remark about my baby, but years later, I realized what the woman meant. My daughter was born an old soul. From the moment she opened her mouth to speak, she was wise beyond her years. She could read at two years old but didn't walk until she was eighteen months old. Sheila was a serious little soul but joyful in quiet moments.

We bonded as only a mother and daughter can do. We were twin souls. She fell ill many times with breathing problems related to pneumonia and her preemie birth. When she was sick, we sat for hours reading books. Sheila nestled in my lap and stuck to me like gum. I loved her with all my heart. That bond is as strong today as it was when she was as small as a kitten. As she grew, my heart ached to watch her count her breaths the way the physical therapist had taught her to do after running and playing. She was so tiny and fragile that it took all her strength just to play with the other children. Each time I saw her struggle for breath in a corner of her room, I would take her into the bathroom and turn the shower on full blast so the steam rising into the room from it would help her get her breathing regulated again.

She was highly allergic to dust, milk, shellfish and animals. When a friend brought her a kitten, we let her keep it despite the doctor's warning. She adored her kitten and named it "Toto" after the little dog in the *Wizard of Oz*.

I worried that she would die during her many bouts of pneumonia when she spent her days and nights in the hospital under an oxygen tent. I couldn't bear to see her so ill and listless, and prayed that she would live to grow into adulthood. When she was in high school, she attended the Athenian School's version of "Outward Bound" and completed the adventure with a three-day solo in the woods of Yosemite, returning healthy and confident. I was so proud. Only Sheila and I knew what an accomplishment that was.

It is said that the soul chooses its parents. There is no question that the souls of my two children chose me.

The Catholic values I'd learned in childhood endured throughout my twenties as a young wife. I still went to Mass and communion almost daily. However, I opened my boundaries beyond my religious background and studiously embraced the religions of the world as I'd done when I first left the convent. The Catholic high school years had shaped my thinking. My ideas of social justice had been cemented by the culture, the nuns and my religious upbringing. I took classes at UC Berkeley and watched my children. I was lucky not to have to work outside the home, but I still held fast to what my parents had taught me so long ago: God created all men (and women) to be equal.

My husband moved up in the banking world. We had plenty of money and lived well. It was a time of snubbing one's nose at the Establishment, but to onlookers, we were now the Establishment. We vacationed in England to introduce our children to London, where their father had been born and had lived as a child. I played tennis at the Country Club, drove a Jaguar and our children had the best of everything.

Still, we protested the Vietnam War and supported the Civil Rights movement. The world seemed upside down and no one was immune to the ideas of the counter-culture revolution.

In 1965, race riots broke out in the Watts area of Los Angeles, with more riots in Detroit in 1967 and Chicago in 1968 where the shattered glass and burning buildings seared our consciousness as we watched the chaos on television. Fear gripped everyone, regardless of race.

Chants of "Hell no, we won't go!" were as commonplace as burning draft cards and American flags. History claims that the Antiwar Movement took root in 1965 when President Johnson began "Operation Rolling Thunder," a massive bombing campaign against the North Vietnamese. In San Francisco, the youth began protesting well before that. These words from the folk song, "Saigon Bride" by Nina Dusheck and Joan Baez fanned the fires:

> "How many dead men will it take
> To build a dike that will not break?
> How many children must we kill

Before we make the waves stand still?"

Amidst the drug culture and the continuing street violence in America, our sons, brothers, fathers and some females went to war. The benefits we reaped were nil. No wonder many Americans were "anti-establishment." We left Vietnam with the guilt of the massacre at My Lai, napalm and the poisoning of our own men from Agent Orange. We wept for our soldiers who were brought home only to be spat upon in the streets for serving their country, or worse, tried for war crimes, tortured as POW's or drug addicted to heroin and marijuana readily available in Southeast Asia.

When I recently visited Vietnam, I was astonished at the limbless citizens (with no hope of prosthetics) who had lost legs or arms due to the landmines left over from the long ago war. I visited the schools established for three generations of the disabled recipients and their offspring of Agent Orange. It breaks my heart as an American to assume responsibility for the dioxin compound poisoning.

During that period, every Friday night a crowd of teenagers gathered by the freeway exit in affluent Orinda, my parents' suburb, hoping to hitch a ride into either nearby Berkeley or all the way into San Francisco for the weekend or longer. My teenage sister, Noreen, hitchhiked to Berkeley. Several weeks went by without any communication from her, and my mother and father were desperate to find her.

I hefted my little son Barry onto my hip, donned my coffee-colored suede fringe jacket, a cotton blouse, embroidered jeans and my chocolate leather Frye boots. I looked just like any other young mother in the area. I brought along a sack lunch for Barry and we scoured the flophouses and druggie hotels in Berkeley. We sat in cafés and became part of the scene. The city was filled with pregnant teenagers and young mothers with small children.

"Reenie, Reenie," Barry called out when he saw a young, red-haired girl wearing a Mexican peasant blouse and flowing skirt, but it wasn't my sister. I couldn't find her anywhere.

Later, I received a lead about a sixteen-year-old who fit my sister's description. She'd moved with a man to the Haight Ashbury district in San Francisco.

Off we went to the Haight. I parked my car a distance away from where I would be walking to look for Noreen so she wouldn't see it and hide. My son and I talked to anyone who would listen. I was invited into communal apartments and houses, but I never found her. Eventually, my adventuresome sister returned to her suburban home life after a few months of drug and sexual experimentation.

I wished I could have used my psychic ability to find her, but I wasn't used to using it for my own concerns. I honestly don't think the notion even occurred to me, and the information that I sought certainly did not "bleed through" into my consciousness. It took years for me to learn the nuances of my own psychic phenomenon, and at that point in my life, I was nowhere near to doing what I can do with it now. At that time, erratic imprints came and went that I couldn't control. My gift is like a muscle in the body, the more it is used and understood, the more finely tuned it becomes, and then it works with more ease.

The habit was that when something or someone was lost or missing in my family, we prayed, "St. Anthony, St. Anthony, stick around. Something's lost and can't be found." (St. Anthony is the Patron saint of lost items). I prayed to find my lost sister, and eventually St. Anthony saw to it that she returned.

The turbulent decade ended with hope. The United States countered its recent past by sending astronauts, Buzz Aldrin and Neil Armstrong on a mission to the moon.

Armstrong as the Commander of Appollo11 was the first man to walk on the moon. Stepping out of the spacecraft, he relayed back to earth his famous quote, "That's one small step for man, one giant leap for mankind."

Chapter 7
1965 – Moraga, California: Visitors

The summer before Barry turned four, my son and I had an experience that made a profound impression on both of us.

My husband was away on business, and Barry and I had spent the evening on the patio enjoying the summer twilight of our small community in northern California's Bay Area. Our house abutted a hillside profuse with vegetation, and some wildlife. We had seen a deer earlier in the afternoon—looking for berries, I presumed. On the hillside above us and visible from our back yard was a series of overhead lines that transmitted electric power on pylons. At the time underground transmission via high voltage cables was not the norm, so it was not uncommon to see electrical power stations. These tall structures were grouped throughout the area.

It was near dark when suddenly, we heard scurrying sounds and the animals in the terrain seemed to be fleeing the area. Then I heard another disturbance. I looked up in the direction of the noise to see a large metal object hovering just next to the series of electrical power lines. I swept my son up into my arms and sat in a patio chair for a long time holding him and watching this spectacle.

What was it? I saw it was round in shape from my vantage point. I took Barry's hand and climbed the hill toward the object. Up close, when we were less than 500 feet away, it appeared more cylindrical in shape and was gunmetal gray in color. Its span was approximately 80 feet in diameter.

Uneducated concerning UFO sightings, I was completely baffled by what I saw. Mesmerized, my son and I watched the craft for at least an hour, wondering if it was some new type of aircraft or helicopter, before it dawned on me that it must be a spaceship.

The craft hovered next to the tower but never touched the ground. Dusk turned to full darkness. We couldn't see the craft any longer, but we could sense a faint pulsation permeating the area, not actually a sound but more a feeling of slight vibration. I went into the house with Barry to call my neighbors to check and see if they had seen the object. Before I did so, I switched on the television. The local news station had been flooded with calls about the strange object hovering near my house. Apparently, everyone within range had seen it.

I remember feeling drowsy and exhausted as I readied my son for bed. I never did call my neighbors that night. The last thing I remember was going into my son's room and sitting on his bed while he changed into his pajamas. I recall he sat with his pajama top on and was getting ready to take off his shorts and put his p.j. bottoms on.

The next thing I knew, it was 5:00 a.m. of the following day and I was awake, fully dressed, and lying next to Barry in his twin bed. He was dressed from the waist down. He still wore his shorts and shoes with the pajamas top he'd donned the night before. I paid scant attention to the strangeness of this at the time, even though it was unusual for me to sleep so heavily. Normally, I'm a light sleeper, but I simply assumed we had both been overtired.

Within a few days, I found myself going to the public library to sift through the newspapers for similar nocturnal sightings. But I found nothing, and I thought it was odd that no reporter had done an article on the object, given the number of calls put in to the local news station.

Shortly thereafter, in 1966, John Fuller published a book about Betty and Barney Hill entitled *Interrupted Journey.* Under hypnosis, they told the story of their abduction by aliens in September of 1961. I read the book from cover to cover. My own earlier sighting of an unidentified craft, coupled with the reading of the Hill's story, triggered a lifelong study of UFO phenomena.

The Hill abduction was considered at the time to be a thwarted kidnapping. This was the first account ever of such an event, and the title—*Interrupted Journey*— seemed a misnomer since what they thought was a kidnapping gone wrong was actually a short-term abduction for a finite period of time and a specific purpose. This fact has been further substantiated through the many remarkable tales of abduction that have occurred since.

The couple was returning home after a holiday in upstate New York and while driving through the White Mountains of New Hampshire, they saw a bright spot of light in the sky. At first, they thought that it was a shooting star, but it ascended rather than descended and halted as it approached the bulging full moon. Betty observed the craft with binoculars as it travelled in front of the moon's surface flashing multi-colored lights. The large craft then plummeted toward the Hills' car. Barney, who was driving, was forced to stop in the middle of the highway. The craft descended to between 70 and 100 feet above the vehicle and filled the Hills' entire field of vision, paralyzing their movements. It was just after this moment that they believe they were lifted into the spacecraft. They were not clear exactly how this occurred.

Barney claimed to have seen eight to eleven alien figures gazing out of the UFO's openings, watching them. The apparent leader continued to watch Barney and gave him the message, "Stay where you are and keep looking."

At the time, Betty sketched a star map indicating Zeta Reticuli as the aliens' home. The galaxy defined as Zeta Reticuli consists of the binary suns, Zeta 1 and Zeta 2 of the constellation Reticulum located approximately 39 light years from us. This galaxy has long been rumored to contain planets with extraterrestrials.

Ten years after my experience, I again researched newspapers in various library archives in California and found that there had been a sighting in Concord, very close to Moraga, within a few days of my experience, but there were no records on file of the sighting near my home.

"Missing time" has now become the standard jargon for an abduction during which time is lost, or an encounter in which nothing is remembered of the time spent aboard a spacecraft until later. Today, writers such as Budd Hopkins, Dr. John Mack, David Jacobs, and others, have kept much better records of the episodes in which people claim to have been abducted and taken aboard a spacecraft. Whether these were actually alien abductions or merely psychological states induced by the psychobiology of the brain is being investigated today on many levels.

Years after I left California, there was a reported UFO sighting in 1997 of nocturnal lights and a craft in Moraga at Sanders Ranch, very close to where I had first sighted a craft in the 1960s. This was thirty years later, and most of the area had been converted to underground utilities. Were they still drawn to the electromagnetic energy of the power stations? Or did they return to follow up on some alien task that we could not decipher due to our limited technology? Was it to connect or re-connect with the human population they had previously contacted?

To this day, Barry remembers the incident he witnessed at almost four years old. As he grew older, whenever he saw a program on television about space, he'd call out to me, "Mom, remember when I was little and we saw the spaceship? Do you think they took us aboard?" As a young adult, he was consumed with television shows such as *Star Trek* and movies like *Star Wars*. He still never misses a scientific rendering of life in outer space as presented by the Discovery Channel.

Several years later through my research, I determined that Barry and I had experienced an "encounter of the first kind." According to J. Allen Hynek, an astronomer and author who first categorized close encounters in his book *UFO Experience: A Scientific Inquiry* (1972) as (CEI), a sighting of an UFO within 500 ft. is an encounter of the first kind. He went on to classify other types of encounters, determining them by the degree of interaction with extraterrestrial life forms. Hynek did not call them aliens or extraterrestrials but referred to them as "animate beings" because as a scientist he was not comfortable with the term "alien."

An encounter of the second kind he associated with physical effects from the UFO such as radiation, catalepsy (human paralysis), and damage to the surrounding terrain such as crop circles. The third type of close encounter he referred to was an actual interaction of some sort with the "animate beings." The fourth type of encounter was human abduction by the UFO or its occupants.

Other researchers such as Jacques Vallee, an associate of Hynek's, argued that the abduction experience should include cases in which there is no physical abduction but there is a transformation of the victim's sense of reality through hallucinatory dreamlike events during the UFO encounters. Later researchers added other categories, fifth—voluntary contactees, sixth—experiences causing death or injury, and seventh—hybrid seeding of human-aliens. These last three classifications extend Hynek's theories but are not widely used and somewhat redundant except for the hybrid mating theory.

Neither my son nor I have any memories after starting to get ready for bed the night of our encounter. Did we have an episode of "missing time"? Or could this incident be classified as an "encounter of the first kind"?

Part 2: DHARMA

Chapter 8
1970s – Dissolution

My marriage disintegrated slowly at first and then with great haste. It was chronologically long enough for me to acknowledge that my husband had what is politely called "a drinking problem." He was an alcoholic. According to AA (Alcoholics Anonymous), it generally takes seven years for the disease of alcoholism to be identified by family members. It took me much longer. It took at least twelve years before I realized that my husband had an addiction and even more time after that to understand that his alcoholism was a disease. The marriage itself lasted seventeen years and another three years after the separation before our divorce was final.

Derek entered rehab on several occasions only to relapse each time. We paid the treatment center ourselves since insurance companies wouldn't pay for rehabilitation back then. My husband claimed that I made him drink, though I barely used liquor myself. It was true that he didn't drink alcohol until he immigrated to America from England and married me, but the responsibility for his drinking lay squarely on his own shoulders.

The children and I attended Al-Anon meetings, but I got very depressed when I realized I was no different from any other spouse of an alcoholic who measured bottles of Beefeater gin to determine how much he had consumed and lied to his secretary for him when he was late for work. "Hi, Jenny, I'm calling this morning to tell you Derek has a dental appointment and will be in later on." Repeatedly, I told lies like this for him while he ate breakfast and tended to his hangover or still slept it off in bed.

I was what was known as an "enabler."

At a Country Club dinner dance one night, I recognized what an imposter I'd become. My husband imbibed freely and was almost comatose when he sat down to eat his dinner and flopped facedown into his salad plate. I calmly stood and bid goodnight to our friends. Then I said, "Come along dear, that medication you're taking doesn't agree with you. I think we'd better leave." There was, of course, no medication; he was dead drunk as I drove us home.

Denial, denial, denial. Without a doubt, denial is the hallmark of the disease, for both the alcoholic and the spouse. I was an expert at it. A few days later a dear friend and neighbor, Rich, said to me, "Your husband needs help."

"For what?" I replied, playing dumb.

Along with the alcohol came the lies and the other women. Under the stress of this dysfunctional marriage, my empathic abilities grew stronger, and I knew he was having an affair with my best friend. I confronted him, and he lied time and again, but I knew. Alcohol abuse spins a web of deceit. No matter how many times I confronted him on the issue of infidelity (not with proof; I had none), he still lied to me every time I asked, yet I knew at my core I was correct in my suspicions.

Whenever I felt extreme distress, my psychic flashes intensified. My dreams were particularly diversified and colorful when my unconscious spoke to me in symbolic imagery. One night when my nerves were frayed, I dreamed of a large circular mandala with the face of my husband's consort—my so-called "friend"—at the center. Next to the mandala was a gravestone. Above the mandala was another set of spirals interlocking one over the other. I studied the mandala with all its colors, wondering what it meant when I heard a shot ring out. I awakened startled and scurried out of bed. Everyone was still asleep. No one but me seemed to have heard the gunfire. When I cautiously checked around, nothing in the house or on the grounds seemed to be amiss.

Several weeks later, I stood at a gravesite. My "friend's" husband had died suddenly. Months after that, I parked our station wagon overnight out on the cul-de-sac and someone shot out the windows with a shotgun. My husband downplayed the incident and had the car taken to the dealer and fixed. He said to me, probably some teenager with a gun out for a joy ride.

When I later recalled the dream, I knew its meaning. The circles interlocking above the mandala represented my marriage spiraling out of control and the grave was that of my "friend's" husband. The gunshots were precognitive and connected to the triangle in my marriage. We never found out who shot the car windows, but I felt I knew who had done the deed.

My stress escalated and I contracted shingles. I scratched the insides of my arms until they bled in my sleep. I had terrible migraines that left me unable to function.

I was filled with a seething inner rage. I thought I'd done everything right, yet my marriage was descending into a hellhole of chaos. I loved Derek and believed that if he stopped drinking, everything would be fine. I never got the chance to find out if that was true or not. My husband never truly stopped drinking the entire time we were married.

During the turbulent 1970s when women's liberation was on the rise, I was also changing. I wanted to finish my degree at Berkeley. We had jointly agreed that I would finish my degree when the children got older. We had set aside tuition money in a separate account for this.

Gingerly, I enrolled first at the community college to study Spanish and parapsychology and find my feet in the world of academia again. I returned to UC Berkeley shortly thereafter. I desired to follow the threads of my psychic visions and studied transpersonal psychology, a discipline founded in the belief that not all psychic experiences can be explained through conventional psychology since it doesn't deal with the altered states of consciousness induced by mystical experiences or psychotropic drugs. Paranormal experiences and abilities are also beyond its scope.

Carl R. Rogers, noted psychologist of the Humanistic Movement, wrote a paper entitled the "Empathic: An Unappreciated Way of Being" which I read. I had often felt that my abilities were unappreciated. His words convinced me that the process of empathy had nothing to do with brilliance and everything to do with a way of being. Being an empath means entering the private perceptions of another and becoming at home in their world. It is a place without judgment. Rogers' early definition of empathy was to "perceive the internal frame of reference of another with accuracy and with the emotional components."

I finally understood why I was drawn to Eastern mystical traditions that tended to transcend the individual self. At the same time, the idea of Jung's "collective unconscious" took hold of me and I had an explanation for the symbols and archetypal concepts that my visions encompassed.

In the two years in which I tried to come to terms with the idea of seeking a divorce, I had a recurring dream. The dream is as clear in my memory today as it was then, and in retrospect, I can't figure out why I was unable to make sense of it at the time. Only when I looked inward through therapy was it clarified.

In the dream, I was with my husband, son, and daughter at Hampton Court in London, England, which we had visited in the past. I entered a maze I'd been in before on several occasions, and I held my daughter Sheila's hand. Time in the dream was current, and Sheila was eight years old. I thought that Barry and Derek had also entered the maze, but I couldn't hear them behind us. I could smell the freshly cut grass outside the maze as well as some unidentified spring blossoms. We started to make our way through the maze leisurely and without fear, believing we'd find the rest of the family and come out on the other side shortly.

However, there was no sign of my husband or son, and Sheila and I seemed to be in the maze alone. We turned to the right. Then we made another right, and after that we turned down one blind alley after another. The hearty shrubs looked like laurel, not the original hornbeam that was planted in the maze. The mixture of greenery seemed as though it was shapeshifting, and I couldn't focus on the way out. I thought following each right turn was correct, but doing that wasn't working.

I called out to my husband and squeezed my daughter's hand to reassure us both. The sun hung lower in the sky, making me realize we'd been in the maze much longer than I had thought.

Suddenly, I heard my son calling to me faintly from a long way off, "Mom! Mother, where are you?" His voice wavered as he asked, "Sheila, are you with Mom?"

I called back but he couldn't hear me and didn't answer. I glanced at my watch, aghast to see that we'd been trapped in the maze for over an hour.

I pulled my daughter close to me. She sensed my emotional distress and began to cry. I tried to calm myself and silently called on our guardian angels to help us find the exit.

The beauty of the maze was gone for me; I no longer liked the shrubs and trees that now loomed like shadowy creatures. The great hanging leaves and branches tricked my mind into thinking that we were about to be swallowed up by English monsters of the night. The sun had dipped even lower, and it was as cold and dreary as only an English day can be.

I couldn't see anyone else, but I heard my son clearly as he sobbed for us to come out of the maze. I couldn't hear his father. Was my son alone?

Taking a sharp left, I saw a pathway. At the end stood a young man and woman who were as distraught as I was. They told me they'd been in the labyrinth for almost two hours. We left when they began to argue with each other. I wanted out of the dark abyss and couldn't wait for them to stop bickering.

Louder, I heard my son yell, "Can you hear me now?"

I yelled back to him.

"You must be closer, I can hear you! Are you okay? Are you with Sheila?" he called, sounding relieved.

"Yes, we're together, but we can't find our way back out."

Collecting my thoughts, I sat on the ground in the maze. It was cold and damp, and I tried to "know" which direction to take to get out of the muddle. Sheila curled into my lap and cuddled me tight. Her small body shivered with cold and fear.

Like an arrow, a light appeared above the pathway to my left. I held Sheila's hand and ran after the dart of light until I saw the exit where my son waited, tears streaming down his face, in the twilight. His father had left him to find us but suddenly reappeared from out of nowhere to chastise us. "You've been in that damn maze for almost three hours, and it's getting dark. What were you thinking? Sheila will catch a bloody cold!"

I was trapped again and again in the dream maze with its thick high walls because they were similar to the imaginary walls of guilt, culture, religion, and fear that trapped me in my marriage. I kept making the same excuses to stay in the marriage and repeated the same methods of madness, hoping for a different outcome. Of course, they didn't work.

Before the dream would dissipate forever, I would have to change the unrealistic belief that my husband would pull himself together and quit drinking because he loved us and didn't want a divorce. I also needed to change my naive expectations.

One lazy afternoon, my husband, who considered himself an expert at barbecuing, was—I thought—preparing the coals, and soon he'd bring the steaks out to the patio to put them on the grill to cook for our Sunday dinner. I couldn't smell the meat, and the side dishes were almost ready, so I walked from the kitchen out onto the patio. I overheard Derek say to Barry, then about thirteen, "Don't the steaks smell great? Look at the charcoal; it's white hot and perfect for grilling."

"Yes Dad, you're doing a great job," Barry replied dutifully.

The meat was on the grill, but the charcoal hadn't been lit. Because his response horrified me, I said rather angrily to my son, "What are you saying? The fire's not lit!" and my sweet child whispered to me "Don't hurt his feelings, Mom. He thinks the meat's cooking. I can cook it for us when he goes into to the dining room to get another drink. I know how, I've watched him do it lots of times."

That was the moment the dream opened up for me. It came to me that our marriage was the maze that trapped me, and I was terrified and unable to find a way out of the situation. Although it had taken months to identify what the maze represented, I had finally pinpointed the meaning of my dream. I was finally able to decide that I would be divorcing my husband, even though he didn't want a divorce and was making it very difficult since he held the power and the purse strings, and I had only the kids, no usable education and no job. Once I called in divine help through my angels—my form of professional help—I was able to come out of the maze of my marriage. The dream stopped recurring after I took back my power and left. I later returned to London to visit but never again went to the maze at Hampton Court.

Several weeks later, my husband put his fist through the glass door of the liquor cabinet because I hadn't replaced his beloved Beefeater gin, and this acted as a catalyst for me. I made appointments to see both a therapist and a divorce attorney.

The day I went to court for the divorce was sad enough, but the stark reality of the era was defined when the judge said to me, "Turn your credit cards in to the court. A divorced, unmarried woman cannot retain her husband's credit." My credit card, standard for the period read, Mrs. Derek W. My name "Susan" was nowhere in sight.

I looked at my attorney, back at the judge, and said slowly and distinctly, "I don't have any of the credit cards. I cut them up." Back in my attorney's office, I confessed that they were still in my purse. I pulled out my credit card to show him the card made out to Mrs. Derek W. I recalled that on a trip to Paris a few years prior, when I made a purchase, the saleswoman had sent me up to the credit department and they wanted not only my passport but to return with my husband and his ID before they would authorize my large purchase. I have never stepped inside that store again on subsequent trips to Paris.

I was so angry that the judge had asked for my credit cards in court that I called the credit card company we dealt with and complained. They offered me a very small limit if I could prove my assets. I owned the house and other monies at the time, which I was going to have to live on. I also had child support.

I didn't like their offer, so instead, I called American Express. To my knowledge, they didn't place the same strict limits on extending credit to females outside of marriage. They agreed to consider giving me credit if I would come to their office in San Francisco and bring some documents.

They wanted to see the divorce settlement and the statement of court-decreed assets along with a copy of the quitclaim deed to the house.

I drove into the city and met with an executive who said he thought he might be able to get me a basic green card, although it was unusual. Humiliated, but defiant, I went home. He called me several days later to let me know I qualified, and I promptly received a card in the mail.

I was so grateful that I used only American Express for nine years. I built up my own credit with them before I ever charged anything on another card. I'm still a loyal customer today. The Equal Credit Opportunity Act of 1974 (Title V and VII Law 93-495) changed the laws giving credit in their own names to single and divorced women who had been denied credit prior to this.

Divorce was one rite of passage I wish I could have avoided. Little was good about being divorced. Now, I was a single mother and the only adult responsible for my children. I lived in affluent suburbia. When I divorced a successful man, it separated me from the rest of the neighborhood. A wall now stood between me and my previous life, my church, and several friends who aligned themselves with the successful husband (who could do them favors, drunk or not) rather than with the difficult woman who had to have a divorce.

I felt that my life was over during the breakup of my marriage. I worried about my children and how they would handle it, and I keenly felt my parents' disapproval over the divorce. My parents adored my husband and would not accept at any time that he was an alcoholic. My father contended at the time that I was crazy to divorce my husband. "Susan, you married him for better or for worse. This is worse. Stay married." After the divorce, my parents watched Derek spiral out of control, and they finally somewhat understood why I did what I did. Yet, upon his deathbed, my father still said to me, "You married Derek for better or worse. You were wrong to divorce him."

I recalled that in the recurring dream, Barry had stood on the outside of the maze with his dad because he couldn't bear to face the reality of his father's alcoholism and tried to view him as normal. He, like his father, remained in denial of the problem. Barry stood by Derek and protected him from my scorn, just as he had when the charcoal remained unlit.

Sheila had been with me inside the maze because she wouldn't go near her father when he'd had too much to drink; she wouldn't sit on his lap or play with him; she was afraid of him. When he was sober, she played with him and gave him all her attention. She vacillated between loving him and being scared of him. My daughter and I were so overwrought by Derek's behavior that we either chided him or ignored him while my son tried to fix him.

These patterns continued for a long time in our relationships with him. Barry rescued him and checked him into hospitals for years, and Sheila hung up on his phone calls or refused to see him when he was drunk. When he sobered up years later, their relationships with him began to change in wonderful ways. At the end of his life, both our children had grown very close to him, and cared for him in their homes. Sheila and Richard in California and Barry and Trish in Arizona took wonderful care of him with hospice assistance before he made his transition to the other side. I kissed him goodbye on the forehead minutes before he died.

Chapter 9
1976 – Evolution

Going from married life to being single was a difficult transition. I missed my husband, my lover and my friend, but at the same time I was relieved not to have to walk the self-destructive path he had chosen with him any longer. The arguing stopped, and it was quiet in our home now.

My children were growing older, and it was a difficult change for them. Our upscale lifestyle came to an abrupt stop. No one else in the neighborhood was divorced, and the neighbors tended to watch my every move. My children could no longer ski at Tahoe, travel, attend camp, or buy trendy clothes most teenagers assume they can't live without. To this day, they remind me that they were the only teenagers on the block who couldn't have TV's in their rooms or private phones (cell phones were a thing of the future). They had food, shelter and love—sufficient enough, I thought. We had a house to live in.

During this period I had an experience that left me unsettled. One night when Barry was about sixteen years old, I went into his room to say goodnight. He was already asleep. As I was about to leave the room, a Chinese dragon (like the one I had seen on parade in San Francisco at Chinese New Year) whirled in front of me and blocked the door. I thought I was dreaming and turned back to check on Barry again. The dragon swished his tail and floated above my son's body for a few minutes. I sat on the bed, but my son didn't awaken. Suddenly the dragon disappeared, and I left the room. I couldn't decipher the meaning of this vision until a few weeks later when I heard my son humming, "Puff the magic dragon that lived by the sea, and frolicked in the autumn mist in a land called Honah Lee. . ." The lyrics sung by folk singers

Peter, Paul and Mary were believed to refer to smoking "pot" although the songwriters, Peter Yarrow and Larry Lipton, denied the reference. I realized then that the dragon had been warning me that my son was smoking pot, and I called him on it. He confessed he was smoking it. This was yet another thing to add to the weight on my shoulders.

I was very fortunate that the house carried a very small mortgage payment. I credit my English husband for disliking to buy on the "hire purchase," meaning that he didn't charge on credit cards or buy things he couldn't afford. While I was married to him, we had no bills other than our house payment. We paid cash for our cars, and we saved regularly. He thought most Americans tended to overspend. After the divorce, I took in a student boarder from a nearby college to help make ends meet, and the children and I survived.

I finished my degree at Berkeley and then attended law school. Using a line of credit backed by home equity and school loans, I managed to pay the tuition. I dated a bit and learned to compartmentalize my life into adult time, law school time, and quality time for my children. My priority was my children, and their teenage years were tough ones for me as a single mother living amongst married neighbors. I made new friends and kept a few of the old. I had a lover who shared my life and helped heal the wounds that had been inflicted by my divorce.

During these challenging years of stress and raising teenagers, I opened up wide and fast psychically. I had visions that I couldn't explain. I attended social functions and "knew" things about people that I did not want to know. Disturbing secrets and sexual orientations would flash into my mind. I was highly uncomfortable when I realized they were emitting from some person I'd just met. My psychic abilities could not be stilled. A young woman I'd met at school had befriended me and always seemed to show up at events I attended. At one such party, I was escorted by a professor friend, Donald. She walked up to us and began a flirtatious conversation with my date. I suddenly had a vision of her nude, engaging in sexually explicit overtures with him while asking me to participate.

The image troubled me, but since I didn't know whether it was my overactive imagination or my psychic ability, I tried to control it and said nothing. Only later did Donald tell me that the woman told him that she wanted to participate in a threesome with us. I declined.

I soon learned that the other person's investment in the emotion or event produced a bleed-through into my psyche. I was an empath, and slowly, with practice, I shut off the unwanted psychic threads. I learned to turn off the images and control the streaming information that flowed into my brain against my will.

Protection of one's psyche is important to an empath. Otherwise, the waking mind will not still and the "reader's" energy will be depleted. I soon learned to put an imaginary circle of light around me to protect me from lower discarnate entities (disembodied souls), who thrive on fear, grief and doubt. They also flourish when the empath is addicted to alcohol, drugs or sex. That's why it is important for a psychic to protect their energetic body and make it difficult for anyone, living or spirit, to penetrate the aura. I never abused alcohol or drugs because, at first, I felt that I was already hallucinatory with my visions, and I couldn't afford to aggravate my condition. Later, I just wanted to keep the channels clearly open. It's also necessary to shield and maintain the physical body with activity, so I tried to stay active at the gym and with the sports I loved--running, skiing and tennis.

I asked the chattering spirits to step away when I didn't want to deal with the information they thrust at me. I learned that it's up to me to decide whether I want a spirit to speak through me (channel) or simply convey telepathic information to me. I have mentored many young psychics, and some believe that because they receive the information, they have a duty to pass it on to strangers, friends, and family. I do not hold to this.

My belief is that psychic mediums' brains are transmitters that broadcast minute electrical signals and electromagnetic waves. In return, we receive many channels, and/or messages, through our "psi" antenna. This allows each of us the option to discern what information we want to disseminate and how we will disseminate it. I don't edit the information that comes to me in any of my readings, but neither do I tell strangers in public places private information just because I know it.

In conjunction with my studies, I enrolled in the Berkeley Psychic Institute and joined their Meditation Group to continue the practice I had begun long ago in the convent. I attended the "Messages from Michael" group in Berkeley and studied transpersonal psychology which by now had gained a strong following in the San Francisco Bay Area. A college friend—who, like me, had children, was about the same age, and was named Susan—and I attended several groups with seekers who channeled information on spiritual topics.

At the UC Berkeley library, there was no "New Age" age category, no books about the lives of the saints such as I had read in Catholic school. Instead, I read Edgar Cayce, Emmanuel Swedenborg, Helena Petrovna Blavatsky, Emma Harding, Sir Arthur Conan Doyle and Eileen Garret in order to gain some understanding of what I was experiencing. The books were grouped under "Occult" back then with books on Quija boards, séances and religious mystics like St Teresa of Avila. Why she was classified under the Occult mystified me.

I began to study my dreams and write them down in a journal. I joined a dream group in Berkeley and later in Virginia and still continue my lifelong study of dreams.

Law school was full of serious students, only one or two of whom had children. Mostly men filled my class. Carolyn was another student who was divorced and had children. We shared our studies and found out that we lived near one another. We became close friends.

A fellow law clerk and friend, Delores, and I investigated the paranormal and expanded our intuitiveness into broader realms. We played with the Ouija board and the pendulum. We took the planchette, and it moved of its own accord without hesitation. It made accurate predictions, both for me and for Delores, concerning our office buddies and our families. Delores, who herself had keen psychic abilities, was as prolific as I was in receiving the messages from discarnate entities on the other side. We visited psychics in San Francisco and in Sacramento who astounded us with their accuracy. Peggy (in Sacramento) told me that I would marry again soon, and I didn't believe it. I had just finalized my first divorce. Eloise (in San Francisco) told me that I would live in a city with cobblestone streets and that the name of that city began with an "A." She also mentioned that I would know the owner of the horse and buggy that plied the streets of my new city. Other more private revelations that later came true changed my belief system concerning these psychics. They often revealed intimate details of my life that no one else could have known.

The first year of law school, I met a man named Charles who drove a Jaguar like I did, but his was a different and sportier model than mine—an XKE. I was trying to sell mine, but it kept breaking down. I had to take it off the market and get it fixed. Charles came over to me during class break one day and mentioned that he'd noticed that we both drove Jags.

"Not for long," I replied. "I'm trying to sell it to help with school expenses."

After that, I saw him in the classroom. He smoked and I didn't take my breaks with smokers, so I only spoke with him on occasion about our cars and school.

One day he took me for a ride in his car. He was quite engaging. He charmed me with stories of his childhood in Wisconsin, his family and his love of restoring old cars. He made me laugh again.

After several months in school, Charles visited me on the job at the Center for Judicial Education and Research in Berkeley. He came into the library where I assisted with writing and researching books for the judiciary. He was tall, so I had to look up at him. The way he looked back down at me, into my eyes, made me know that we would be together.

Charles worked several blocks away and began to drop in to have coffee with me in Berkeley. He was seeing someone else then, but it wasn't long before he ended it.

We began to spend time together at his place in San Francisco. This was often difficult to achieve since I had to be home for my children and attend to their needs, so after awhile he moved in with us. We told my children he was just a roommate (I rented him my spare room), but eventually we confided in them that we were lovers.

He was twelve years younger than I was, and what we both thought would simply be a wonderful friendship turned into a serious love affair. I think it caught us both off guard. I know that I had no intention of re-marrying and liked the ease of the relationship up until that point.

We were a very good match; he calmed my intensity, and I learned to relax more through his example. He would lie around on Saturdays watching cartoons and cooking shows—even though he only ever cooked lasagna—while I was out running errands, or at the grocery store or studying.

Charles and I had the same interests: old cars, fast cars, antiques, gourmet dining, good friends, gardening, books and the law. He was a homebody and he suited me.

We married after he graduated from law school. I loved him with all my heart.

His only faults were that he smoked and was a master at procrastination. I always did and still do everything I need to do well in advance or first thing in the morning, my theory being that several new tribulations will appear that I will need to deal with immediately, so it's best to have as much out of the way as possible. I made a list every morning and didn't go to bed until I had checked off each item on the list. (I must confess that I have since let go of this habit and now consider anyone who is as neurotic as I was to be plain crazy).

Chapter 10
1982 – Suicide

It was the first weekend I could remember in several years that I'd actually been alone with a man without my children in tow. Law school, my new lover, and my children were taking a toll on my psyche. I was mentally and physically exhausted even though things were calmer once Charles moved in with us. On a lark, we flew to Phoenix to spend a weekend with his widowed aunt. For awhile after I got there, I immersed myself wholly in the present, no thoughts of school or children. I completely forgot for the weekend that I was a mother, but it wasn't long before I began to have troublesome feelings regarding my own mother.

Mom had agreed to stay with Barry. (Sheila was away at boarding school at the time, paid for by a line of credit from my house). She had recently moved into our house, so I believed my son could not have been in safer hands. The long weekend away had been wonderful, but a small, nagging feeling kept me from fully enjoying my freedom. I kept worrying about my mother because she'd grown anxious and depressed. I was concerned about how she'd fare when dealing with my teenage son.

Barry could be a pain because he had a habit of bringing everyone he met to the house. Sometimes, it was a bit too much, like the time he invited a runaway girl who'd been living in a gas station to our home. As she ate the dinner we shared with her, she bragged that her father was head of the Klu Klux Klan for the area where they lived in rural Tennessee.

"Charles did you hear that?" Horrified, I choked on my food.

My partner—who normally was as liberal as I was—ended the dinner, saying, "We have a present for you. Get on the phone to your parents and tell them you're coming home."

We made the girl phone her parents immediately. She left for home the next morning via a bus ticket we could ill afford. At the time, I had actually never met anyone with such a narrow-minded point of view. I had long been a resident of California where differences are the tolerated norm. However, tolerating a member—even one once removed—of the Klu Klux Klan was too extreme even for our thinking. I worried Barry might bring some other unsuitable acquaintance home to his grandmother.

She had recently taken Barry and his friend Simon out to lunch on a high school holiday and she commented to me, "I had a wonderful time with the boys at lunch. They laughed and giggled like girls. They made me laugh too. I so enjoyed them and watched them as they ate two desserts each of chocolate cake and big pieces of berry pie with ice cream, *after* they had already eaten cheeseburgers. Can you imagine? We had such a magical afternoon."

Of course, when I quizzed Barry later, he confessed they had smoked a joint before she had invited them to lunch and were pleasantly high. My mother evidently thought the "munchies" were an admirable trait.

Barry used to complain to me that he was the only one who ever got in trouble at school amongst his classmates because he would tell the truth about the incident and the others would lie. However, I appreciated his honesty.

Mom hadn't been herself since she had moved in just before Christmas, and her "poor pitiful widow" attitude cast a pall over the house. Charles, a CPA prior to law school, had gone over her finances countless times and assured her she was solvent, but she constantly worried about money, the future and all seven of her grown children.

She was clinically depressed, but I'd never seen anyone in the depths of this kind of despair and didn't recognize the severity of her disease. She voiced her fears to me, saying repeatedly, "Susan, I took a wrong turn off the freeway." What did this metaphor refer to? What mistake did she perceive she'd made that I couldn't fathom?

She had bought and sold real estate after my father retired and had done quite well. She had a home up on the Mendocino coast that she thought she wanted to live in. It was fully paid for. Her income included pensions, social security and savings, and was "comfortable." My father had died eighteen months prior, and no doubt she missed him. However, she seemed to enjoy her newfound freedom and did spend time here and there with her friends. We took her to the family doctor, and he prescribed an anti-depressant.

I was as anxious driving home as I had been at the airport in Phoenix where I had difficulty choosing a small gift for Mom. I had a knot in the pit of my stomach. My funds were skimpy because I worked for the Judiciary while in school, which on the work-study program paid $4.50 per hour, not much with two children to feed. I couldn't spend much and that added to my feeling of doom, but honestly, I wandered from shop to shop and finally picked out a jar of cactus jelly made in Arizona. It looked slimy, and I doubted anyone would ever eat the junk. Why had I purchased that item when I knew she loved peanut brittle, a treat that was available in every shop? I couldn't ward off the ominous feeling I had, but attributed it to being away from home and outside my usual hectic schedule.

I voiced my anxiety to Charles as we stepped into the house. I called out my mother's name but she didn't answer. Her car was parked in front of the house, so I assumed one of my siblings had come to collect her and take her out to dinner or over to their house. My son was at work, and when he got home, he asked, "Where's Grandma? She was here this morning."

At that moment, the phone rang. It was Eddie, my little brother, who was living, working and going to college in San Francisco at the time. "Hi Susan, Ed here. Where is Mom? I've been trying to reach her all day. I called all the others, except Noreen. When I couldn't get hold of Noreen, I even had the police drive by her place, and Mother wasn't there. It scared Noreen to death."

"Ed, Mom's car is parked outside, so someone must have picked her up. Maybe she's gone to dinner or to a movie with a friend."

I told Ed that Barry and I had searched the backyard (which was extensive) and had walked the path through the redwood trees. We had opened the gate at the property line and searched the woods beyond it to no avail. I called my neighbors to ask whether she was at one of their homes or if anyone had seen her. I again called my older brother who lived nearby to see if Mom had shown up at their house. At first, we thought there must be some logical explanation, but as the night wore on, our anxiety mounted.

Ed and I both felt something was terribly amiss, yet he claimed he wasn't "intuitive" like his sisters. Something was drastically wrong. I knew it, and my brother knew it. We phoned each other back and forth all night trying to reassure ourselves, but my baby brother and I worried the night away thinking, "What if she's dead?"

I never slept that night in February. Charles humored me, but after awhile he went back to sleep when I kept repeating, "Something's wrong. Something's wrong."

At 6:00 a.m. the next day, I took a shower and readied myself for work. I called my sister Ananfaye and asked her to drive over to my house.

"Yes, I'm on my way," she said. She never complained that she had to get to work, that it was too early, or that the drive was too far: she said, "Yes," because she also knew something wasn't right.

When the sun was on the rise, I went outside to look again in daylight for my mother before I had to leave, thinking perhaps she'd fallen out by the redwoods in the backyard and was hurt. Maybe we'd missed her when we'd looked last night. I stumbled around in the shrubbery. I stood under the birch trees and walked the path to the fence behind the redwoods. No one was there.

It was quiet, too quiet; I turned to assess the silence. The pool equipment had been turned off and the pool sweep wasn't rotating around the pool, something I'd missed in the dark.

Alarmed, I stood by the swimming pool looking into a surge of cloudy blue water. I couldn't see the bottom. All I could see was the unfamiliar blue haze.

In a flash, I knew that my mother was dead and lying at the bottom of my pool.

I could look no further; I ran inside and went into my mother's bedroom. Neatly laid out on her nightstand was a pair of glasses and her rosary. Her purse sat on the dresser. I opened it to find her wedding ring in its original box inside. I'd never before seen the ring box with the Oregon jeweler's name stamped on the outside.

"Barry, Charles, come quickly!" I cried, running back to the pool again.

"Mom, what's wrong?" My son heard the panic in my voice and came outside. He took the long-handled mesh pool skimmer from my hands and probed the cloudy blue water.

"Mama!" I screamed when I saw her tied to a decorative wrought iron patio chair at the bottom of the pool. We stood for what seemed eons and stared at the figure clad in a light blue fleece bathrobe, which had leaked dye into the pool, coloring it the blue of a robin's egg. The chair was also blue; I had painted it that color myself last fall.

What had happened? Did she fall and panic? Did she try to frantically kick her legs and swim back to the surface? No; I looked down to see that her legs were tied with rope.

She had tied her arms and legs to the chair, knowing that she wouldn't be able to change her mind and save herself; that she would drown because she couldn't use her arms to untie the knots she had fashioned. My mother knew how to make sailor's knots because she'd grown up on Prince Edward Island, a Maritime island off the coast of Nova Scotia. She was quite familiar with boats and the sea. She was an excellent swimmer and taught each of us to swim when we were quite small.

When all the air had left her lungs and she began to inhale water, did it burn her throat and lungs? She hadn't talked or tried to scream, that I know for sure; it would have taken all her strength just to breathe.

I couldn't speak. My own breath was suspended, stalled as an airplane stalls in flight. Only with deep inhalation did it return in short gasps. The horror of the scene before me imploded in my brain. It was several moments before I was able to scream, "Who did this to her?"

Could she see the surface, feel the weight of the armature around her, and did she gasp for air and struggle for life? Or, dear God, did she close her eyes and give in to death willingly?

Charles was on the phone, dialing 911. I could hear the tension in his voice as he struggled to remain calm. "We have a drowning, please hurry! Yes, I'm sure."

Charles gave the dispatcher the requested information, and in minutes the response team filled our backyard.

A fireman asked, "Son, do you know this woman? Can you tell me who it is?"

"That's my grandmother in the pool." Barry identified her body. I had gone back inside. No one asked me who she was, and I didn't go back out while they were there. I could not. I regret that they left the deed of identifying my mother to my son. It was too much to ask of a boy.

We never knew how she'd managed to tie herself up, whether her arms were tied together or separately to the chair. I don't remember discussing this with the firemen who untied her prior to calling the police.

In any case, the police investigation established that she had indeed been able to tie herself up sufficiently with knots that would be difficult to untie. They also ascertained that she had jumped to her death from the diving board into the pool.

The police further checked with my mother's doctor who concluded that she had been clinically depressed. Mom had also emptied her safety deposit box, and we found her personal papers on the dresser in her bedroom, including her will. The police concluded their investigation and determined that there was no hint of foul play. The coroner ruled her death as a suicide. However, one of her sisters, as well as my siblings, Noreen and Ed, insisted for a long time afterward that someone had murdered her.

That day and the days that followed are not a blur, as are other events of my life that I can only partially recall. No, the words spoken that day are imprinted in large point, bold font on my memory's monitor. The scenes replay themselves in periodic flashbacks that contort like dancers in a music video.

I was left behind, to survive another day wounded with grief, sorrow, guilt—and later, anger. The day of the funeral, at my mother's gravesite, was the last time I shed a tear for years to come.

My sister Noreen and I sliced the valium pills my doctor had given me into pieces and split them between us so we could maintain our grip for a few days. Instead of black, I wore a teal blue silk fitted dress with long sleeves to the funeral. My mother had paid for the dress. I had needed something special for an occasion, and she wanted to get it for me because she knew I hadn't bought myself any new clothes in quite awhile. Wearing it was my way of honoring her memory.

Graveside, each of us seven siblings placed a white rose on the coffin before it was lowered into the fresh-turned earth. I began to wail and sob uncontrollably. It took a long time to pull myself together.

My mother's suicide carved indelible scars upon my heart that penetrated the core of my survivor's existence. I was angry at her choice. Why hadn't she talked to any of her children about her feelings? What other fears haunted her? She thought she had no money when in fact she had enough to live very well. She had recently retired at age sixty-five. Did she feel useless and old? Had that played a role in her decision?

I tormented myself. Had she tried to tell me, and I just hadn't listened? Or, had I heard the plea and ignored the message? Why hadn't she left a suicide note? (That seemed odd since she was an excellent writer and often wrote notes to us)

My rage was also directed at God. My good Catholic mother had said her rosary before she drowned herself from what we could tell. Where was her God (and mine) when she prayed?

My mother had seven children, abstaining from the use of birth control in accordance with the rule of Rome. I believe having so many children was emotionally too much for her to handle over the years. I can still hear her laughing as she joked, "I had my seven children. If the Pope changes the rules, I'll be marching on Rome for compensation." But was it really a joke to her?

Woefully, I remember the woman who stayed married to my father but fantasized about leading another life, a mother who was smart and funny, who loved to laugh and wear pretty clothes. My father called her his "Irish princess" and loved her with all his heart, but his adoration never seemed to be enough.

My mother was a creative genius. She could draw a dress, make the pattern from newspaper, pin the pieces onto the fabric and cut them out, and then sew those pieces together to make a fabulous creation for any one of her five girls. She cut our hair and gave us perms copying pictures from magazines, reconstructing the latest hairstyles. She saw trends long before anyone else did, and she incorporated them in her world of home, cooking, and fashion.

She had business ideas galore. She also loved to buy and sell real estate and never passed up the opportunity to view an open house.

I think of her fortitude. When my father had a stroke at age fifty-nine and was disabled by it, she went out to find a job but no one would hire her. She had no experience because she'd stayed at home raising children. She applied to J.C. Penney's department store, thinking she knew quite a bit about children's wear. She was denied the job at Penney's and received a refusal letter citing her lack of experience.

My mother was crushed. She argued to me, "But I do have experience! I have seven children. I can look at a child and know his or her size—from toddler to teenager—in an instant. I can even tell you their shoe size. I know what materials last and how to find the most value for the money." She told me that she had expected to get the interview and thought that she could then explain her experience, but since she couldn't talk to them in person, she couldn't prove she could do the job.

"Mom, answer the letter and tell them that," I told her.

In a letter to the Human Resources Department, my mother wrote her succinct argument, and the gentleman who had denied her the position called her immediately for an interview. He offered her the job at the end of the meeting, and she was elated.

Regardless of all that she had going for her, the fact remains: she killed herself at my house, in my pool, in my beloved "garden" where my teenage son found her.

My vulnerable heart joined in marriage with Charles the same year my mother committed suicide even though I wasn't sure I wanted to be married. I knew I loved him, and I definitely needed him. The psychic that I had seen in Sacramento was correct; I remarried much sooner than I had ever dreamed I would.

My mother's death created a chasm of loss within me. Not only was she gone, but the part of me that was Clara's child was forever lost, too. I had another crisis of faith similar to those I'd gone through when I gave up my vocation with the nunnery and when I'd gone through my divorce. The loss of my parents stunned me into accepting that I was now an adult orphan.

After my divorce, I'd given up on going to church. I had cried through every service despite my Jackie O. sunglasses, and my children were upset by it. Now, in my bereavement, I gave up on God completely. I raged against Him, I mocked Him, I scorned Him and I hated Him in the depths of my soul for allowing my mother to commit suicide.

The unnerving psychic episodes I'd had during the period of my extreme stress and divorce re-surfaced. I was jumpy, and every nerve ending was on alert. After the funeral, I began to lose everything I ate, projectile vomiting like a baby. I couldn't keep anything in my stomach. I lost weight and struggled to feel better. It took medication and therapy to stabilize my body and regain my equilibrium. I heard conversations in people's heads, knew what I could not know, and worked hard to turn off the visions.

Psychic attacks hit me at the oddest moments. The more I thought about the suicide, the more I opened to negative forces and my body responded in kind. I was weakened mentally, and physical exhaustion opened me to lower astral entities. I had to refute the spirits around me by calling in beings of light to counter the negativity of the suicidal thinking that was not mine, but my mother's.

I was aware that dark spirits, lower astral entities, and negative thought forms could move into a physical body and its aura to affect what the host thought, spoke, desired and felt. This invasion could alter the person's behavior, and as the entity continued to occupy the body of the individual, apparent personality changes could occur. I knew all of this, and yet I continued to dwell on the suicide, bringing on further attacks.

I believe some psychic attacks involve the intentional manipulation of spirits through induced spells, voodoo, negative energy rays, black magic and the like. Other entities simply find their way into debilitated psyches that are weakened by illness, chemicals, drugs or alcohol. I was not actually ill once the vomiting was under control, and I wasn't using drugs or drinking alcohol at the time, but I was mentally susceptible.

One moment, I'd be happy and productive, and then, all of a sudden, I would be filled with fury at God, demanding to know why He had allowed my mother to kill herself. I had absorbed my mother's rage. For days, I would drag around, filled with fatigue for no apparent reason. I sensed someone or something watching me. Anger and fear colored my thinking; I was afraid for my children's future and adopted a fretful, worrywart attitude that I had never before experienced.

Like a beacon for the underworld, my chakras and energy field flashed with distorted black light. I had to use everything that I had learned to right myself again. I worked on properly spinning my chakras at the perfect speed and closing any holes that had been opened in my aura.

These examples might all seem like they're common reactions to any life-changing event, not just suicide, but they were different for me. Although I had experienced several life-altering experiences, I had never faced this type of phenomena. The rage, fear, and anxiety were magnified beyond anything I had ever dealt with before. I didn't recognize myself during periods of fear of the tiniest proportions. If my bank account balance dropped to ten dollars, I was convinced I would never have another dime. When I got upset for any reason, my ire caused me to say unthinkable things to the people I loved.

I prayed for strength to release the negativity. I visualized gathering all of it into my solar plexus, mentally attaching it to the area with a simple silver cord. I envisioned all the miniscule fears and worries being broken up with a laser of white light and dissolving into the cord, so that they would be released into the center of the earth when I untied the cord.

As a medium, I was aware that though my mother had crossed over, she was still in torment and not yet free of angst. I prayed to the angelic realms to lift me away from her misery. I knew the emotional distress I felt was not mine, and I had to concentrate on restoring my own psychic equilibrium. I took sage and burned it throughout my house even though it made me cough and wheeze.

I finally cleared my aura and the psychic attacks subsided. I had lost seventeen pounds in six weeks, but I was the old me again, only skinnier.

Like any form of forgiveness, forgiving my mother's choice was a long road filled with potholes. Sometimes, the potholes could be maneuvered around in the barely visible road, and other times, I'd sink into a pothole unawares and be unable to crawl out for awhile.

Why couldn't I fathom her choice? Some days, I believed that in her chemically imbalanced brain, she must have thought that suicide was the best choice she could make. Other days, I failed to comprehend her thought patterns. Her creative ability to think outside the box and dream the impossible only strengthened my conviction that, at that moment in time, she must have been gravely ill.

Charles and I had a business dinner party a few months later, in an effort to get on with life, I suppose. That night, the attorneys we had invited discussed at length an estate case in which both decedents had drowned in an accident together. It was critical to pin down the sequence of the drownings in order to administer the estate according to inheritance laws. This was a key issue because the couple both had children from previous marriages. The chronology of the deaths of the decedents would determine who would inherit and when.

The dinner conversation moved on to the experts and what they would testify to regarding the stages of drowning if the case went to trial. This discussion sticks in my brain as though it was yesterday. Charles was the only one who knew what I had recently lived through, and he couldn't get them to change the topic.

One attorney named Jon had laboriously studied drowning from a medical point of view and wanted us to hear all he had learned. He diligently recounted the stages to us one by one. "First," he explained, "there's surprise. In this stage, the victim recognizes danger and is afraid. He/she assumes a near-vertical position in the water, with little or no leg movement. Arms are at or near the water's surface, making random grasping or flipping motions. Head is tilted back with the face turned up. Victims rarely make any sounds; they're struggling just to breathe."

Yes, right, I thought, *tie your arms with rope and see how well they flail.*

"Second, the body drops below the static water line and, in an attempt to protect itself, involuntarily holds the breath. This occurs because water has entered the mouth and caused the epiglottis to close the airway. Though the victim may continue to struggle, no noise is made because he/she can't breathe.

"The third stage is loss of consciousness. Because the victim has been without oxygen, the body shuts itself down. In this stage, the victim is motionless. He/she goes into respiratory arrest. There's no chest movement or breathing sounds. At this point, the victim sinks to the bottom of the water, either slowly or rapidly, depending on factors such as the amount of air trapped in the lungs, body weight, and muscle mass. Unconsciousness will lead to death unless breathing is re-established."

I covered my face with my hands and tried not to look at anyone at the table. Charles winked at me and got up from his seat across from me on some pretense. He stood behind my chair, caressing my hair and touching the nape of my neck.

Jon paused for effect before he continued, "Due to lack of oxygen to the brain, the victim might look as though he/she is having a convulsion, which is why the next stage is called the hypoxic convulsion stage. The victim's lips and fingernail beds turn blue and the body either goes rigid or violently jerks. There can also be frothing at the mouth."

(Thank God my son was at work that day!)

He continued, "The final stage in the drowning process is death. Clinical death occurs when both breathing and circulation stop. The heart stops pumping blood. The victim is now in cardiac arrest. The vital organs no longer receive oxygen-rich blood. The lack of oxygen causes the skin to turn blue."

I learned more about drowning from a technical standpoint than I ever wanted to know.

Dessert was crème brûlée, made with fresh vanilla beans which I had carefully scraped from the pod. Today, even the faintest whiff of vanilla always throws me right back to that dinner party and the drowning lesson.

Somehow, I made it through the evening. Once all our guests left, I went into my bathroom. My chest felt as though someone had sat on it, my skin was clammy, and I was sweating profusely. The conversation had caused visions of my mother's drowning to lodge like heartburn in my chest. I bent over the toilet and expelled the pictures from my mind as forcefully as I did the dinner that roiled in my stomach.

Chapter 11
1988 – Miami, Florida: Transition

I left my second husband. We did our own divorce, and I left even though I loved him. I can't say why, except that I wanted to live out loud. Nothing worked for me anymore. I ran away.

In retrospect, I can see that the grief over my mother's suicide was not yet resolved within me. I wanted out of my life filled with commitments. My children were now young adults, and I wanted to be free. Charles and I had been together almost a decade. He once said to me while we were still in law school, "When we finish law school, you will find me boring." I never actually found him boring, but he was a homebody. I wanted to investigate other cultures, other relationships, and travel. I wanted to delve into all that the world had to offer. I felt confined, restrained, like I was missing some huge global party that I felt compelled to attend. He wanted to be successful and make partner at his law firm. Honestly, sometimes I thought I was doomed to marry men whose success brought about a metamorphosis that transformed them from wonderful, loving partners into avaricious, ego-driven androids.

Before I left California, I stayed for several months with my sister, Noreen, and her daughters, Natalie and Angelina, up in the Sonoma wine country. Noreen and I spent hours and hours in conversation, laughing until we cried. We were so rowdy, Natalie yelled, "Please, please shut up! I can't sleep! Stop talking!" I don't know how we made it to work the mornings after we'd talked the night away. We took long walks though the vineyards adjacent to her house. Brimmed hats and sunscreen protected our fair Irish skin. Noreen wore white gloves to keep her hands from freckling.

The experience was a catharsis for me and healed me in ways that only being with family can.

South Beach was in renovation. Art Deco design signatures replaced the soft pastels of the buildings that jutted out on the avenue, identifying the district. Ocean Drive was widened to accommodate the refurbished homes of its tenants. Curved hotel facades decked out in new paint abutted buildings disheveled by time. Cobalt blue neon lights winked under window frame eyebrows. Tinted hues and stucco white juxtaposed with the newly painted mauves and browns that now bedecked a corner club. The low-rise streetscape was lined with outdoor cafes, the tables of which were filled with suntanned bodies in skimpy swimwear. Crack addicts mingled with beach boys, retirees, and *Marielitos*—Cuban ex-cons shipped to Miami from Mariel Harbor outside Havana in the 1980s at Castro's consent—in dirty jeans. Rollerbladers navigated the construction tiers as they headed north on the sidewalk. Coconut oil, *ganja*—marijuana—and sweetened body odors permeated the balmy night air.

Further up the road, an old man sat outside on the porch of a small hotel on a weathered beach chair, watching as his home fell prey to the wrecking ball of change.

Adjacent to this dilapidated building, a once-proud house sat back from the street, its majestic wooden doors now worn, and their peeling paint covered in dirt and grime. Remnants of a black wrought iron fence with tines that stuck up from the sand like twisted strands of giant black licorice barely held together a scrollwork gate that creaked when the wind blew in from the sea. From the wide portal of its courtyard, the house overlooked the Atlantic Ocean and a carpet of sandy shore. Just inside the gate, a young woman sat amongst the tangled weeds embedded in the sand reading tarot cards for her customer. The two hunched over the spread, her client spellbound by fate.

In its crumbling splendor, the Mediterranean-style *casa* hinted at a former opulence that would have surprised the seedy occupants who now stumbled through its battered doors. One could see from the east side of the street into the upstairs window where a dim light cast shadows on a spiral staircase as it wound its way up to a series of dingy second and third floor rooms for rent. It was a crack house then, but slowly the neighborhood gentrified. Eventually Gianni Versace bought it, renovated and added onto it, before he was murdered right in front of it. The year was 1997, and he had just left the News Café down the street. By then the place had been turned into a mansion, and the property was priceless.

Across the street at the beachside park, palm trees bowed to the ocean breeze and scattered sand as they bent. A large oval clock on the crumbling pavilion was stopped at 10:10 p.m. No moon was visible, and the sky hung dark and silent, breaking at the horizon where the ocean sounds began.

Jazz escaped from the Edison Hotel, eager to spill out on the sidewalk. Neon lights flashed and winked at pedestrians. The outdoor barstools at the Clevelander were filled with multi-colored bodies twined together like strands of variegated rope. European voices mingled with Latin accents as the speakers vied for attention; locals, models, gigolos and a few businessmen from out of town posed like actors on a movie set.

South Beach, like me, was in transition. This was where I landed when I moved on to Miami with its tropical nights filled with music and laughter and days full of sunshine and waves. Living there was like living in a foreign country except that nearly everyone spoke English. My son drove my car cross-country for me and stayed with me in my new home for several weeks while he was on winter break.

I had stepped away from all that was familiar, and it wasn't long before I felt that life had duped me. I perceived that I had followed the whisperings of my spirit and "got fucked." The job I had moved for fell through. The man I had also come to Miami to embrace slipped through my fingers. I was left alone to live in a beachfront hotel on unemployment. When my checks ran out, I had to decide whether to stay or go back to California. I had left my job there, and my son and daughter. Filled with loss, I reached the lowest point in my life.

The next job offer I received was ideal for me—teaching criminal law to Miami Police Officers. However, the day of my last board interview, I went out to play with a friend from out of town and missed the interview. They called to tell me that I was their number one candidate, and I blew it because I failed to show up. This was so unlike my responsible self that I cried myself to sleep that night.

My youngest sister Gloria had recently divorced and she and her new boyfriend Lance decided to move from California to Florida. The three of us pooled our money so we could share a large apartment in North Miami. Gloria was a professional model, and she had acquired a lucrative job offer with a Miami agency. She too, had been lured to the city by the promise of sunshine and a better life, but her job fell through right after she arrived. We both began life anew in Miami without money, jobs or friends. Gloria's life intersected with mine during a time of crisis for us both. We came together unsure of what to expect next in our lives.

At that time, Miami was full of people who had left their old lives to start anew. Lawyers and doctors from overseas held under-the-table service jobs so they could live simply on the beach. The city was a big party community. Lance was the only one of us who had a job. I did hold some psychic readings out of bookstores and at fairs and whatever else I could to earn a few extra dollars, but mostly, I played hard until both my unemployment checks and my savings ran out. I met a new man named Carlos, and we spent hours riding our bicycles, rollicking on the beach, and doing nothing. He called it "the art of being."

Chapter 12
1988, 1989 — Sisters

Outside the temperature dropped. The winds reached near
hurricane levels. On the west coast, it would have been
Indian summer. In south Florida, it was hurricane season, and
we were on alert. Hurricane Gilbert had devastated Jamaica,
but the West Indians believed that Mother Earth, in her fury,
had cleansed the "bad magic" from the island. The sun came
out again and it was hotter than before even though it was the
time of year when it was supposed to be cooling down.

Gunshots in Tiananmen Square resounded around
the world. The People's Liberation Army rolled in with tanks,
and the Chinese government gave the order to murder its
protesting citizens. How many had died? No one had the
count.

The Berlin Wall echoed the cry of the dying and
crumbled. Social disorder erupted across several continents.
Citizenry watched immobile and speechless in front of their
television sets, every change of the channel merely brought a
different country's hostilities into focus. The decade ended
with a violence that resonated within me because there had
been a vicious erasure of what I considered to be "normal,"
of what I believed to be real and true, in my life.

I was still unable to truly grieve the loss of my mother
or come to terms with her suicide. I missed Charles even
though it had been my choice to divorce him. I missed my
friends and my children in California. Sheila was living in a
dorm at college and Barry was working and living in an
apartment with roommates.

While the three of us—Lance, Gloria and I—were
living together, Gloria had an experience that I was witness
to. I became her caretaker during a bizarre, three-day period

in which she regressed to the womb. She acted like a newborn baby, and then a toddler, a child, and a young adult. I watched her undergo these regressive yet progressive stages with my own eyes. At the end of the experience, she was transformed into a changed woman, both emotionally and spiritually.

It all began when we had been living together for only a few weeks. Lance was away at work and the two of us women were alone in the apartment one pre-dawn morning. My sister stood in front of the mirror in her bathroom trembling with pain. As she glanced into the mirror, she saw clearly her own brown eyes, but in the whites of them was the image of an Asian woman, holding her hands to her cheeks, staring back at her. The woman wore a white lab coat. Gloria shook her head to ward off the apparition, but the image stood firm. The pain swept over her entire body and inched its way up the back of her neck, freezing her posture in place. Pain lanced through the instep of her right foot until she cried aloud.

Gloria stumbled into the living room where she could see the panoramic view of the inter-coastal area. She knew this would comfort her. Sailboats and powered yachts meandered aimlessly, piercing Miami's skyline with their glistening masts of chrome and steel.

I was in my bedroom at the far end of the apartment when she called out to me, "I can't breathe, Susan!" I rushed to her side, and she asked, "What is wrong with me? I don't want to spend the rest of my life in a chiropractor's office because of my back. That has to be what's causing this terrible pain I'm in." She told me about the strange vision she'd had of the Asian woman.

Gloria had sustained injuries in a horrendous fall. Although her back had healed somewhat since then, she still had periods of pain and difficulty. She began to sob as memories of her accident flooded her consciousness. "I can't take this anymore!" she cried.

"You'll be okay. Don't cry. You need to see a doctor," I told her.

"We've only been in Miami for three weeks; we don't know any doctors."

"A friend of mine mentioned an acupuncturist— a Dr. Shih. That's it! Let's get you an appointment with her."

I walked over to the sliding glass door and opened it. I could see whitecaps frothing the surface of the water below. Red and yellow hibiscus petals fluttered over the wrought iron railing from potted ceramic jars. The humidity had dropped, and autumn's breath filled the room, reviving my ailing sister.

"Acupuncture's the thing to try first. It releases blocked energy throughout the body, clears the meridians and allows your natural energies to flow, relieving the pain. It worked for me when I had neck problems several years ago. In fact, it was miraculous."

"But don't they use needles—long needles?" Gloria grimaced.

I managed to overcome her objections, and as we entered the building, the sign on the door read, Whei Shih, O.M.D., C.A. Gloria and I stepped inside to the smell of herbs. Within minutes, a tiny Chinese woman introduced herself and chatted a few moments with my sister about her symptoms before she felt her pulse.

She told Gloria, "Your liver is like a teapot ready to boil over. Your spleen is also affected. You have what we in Chinese medicine call a 'hot' liver."

After the session, Gloria told me what had happened in the patient room. She disrobed and lay on the working table. Dr. Shih inserted several needles into her neck and back. Her skin never broke and no blood escaped. The pinpricks she barely felt left long protruding needles rising upward in the air. The room was filled with the pungent odor of Chinese herbs. Fear gripped my sister when she tried to release a yawn and instead began to choke and gag.

"Don't be afraid. I can help you." Dr. Shih sat lovingly with her for over an hour while the aroma of the herbs combined with their medicinal effects soothed the pain in her body.

While I sat in the waiting room, the needles were removed and my sister put her street clothes back on slowly. The herbal air that filled her lungs made her feel dizzy, but her limbs moved easily and without pain.

As Gloria paid the bill, she glanced across the desk into Dr. Shih's office. She saw a small woman turned slightly, holding her hands to her face. The whiteness of the doctor's jacket leapt out at her and she knew that Dr. Shih was the Asian woman she had seen in the mirror the morning she'd had her vision.

That session eliminated her acute pain. She continued to see Dr. Shih who prescribed an herb patch to be taped to her back for several days, a series of acupuncture sessions, and Chinese herbs taken orally with Coca-Cola every day. Within a few weeks, Gloria noticed a marked improvement in her health, and the pain was gone. After that, her standard advice whenever one of us was feeling under the weather was to half-jokingly tell us to drink Coke and drop in the magic Chinese herbs. "Whether you can read the Chinese label or not, Dr. Shih's miracle cure will make you feel better immediately." (We never figured out if the curative effect came from the Coca-Cola or the Chinese herbs).

After Gloria began to feel better, she had another strange episode. She stepped into the shower and began to hum, but then she choked and gagged and the words of the song were lost as she sputtered.

I was in the kitchen making our morning coffee when she raced from the bathroom clad in only a towel, trying to speak but unable to form a word. Coughing, retching sounds escaped as she covered her mouth with her hands. I thought she was having some kind of anxiety or panic attack that left her unable to speak.

She leaned against me and rasped, "Something is inside of me trying to get out!"

Sweat poured from her ashen face and her dark hair hung in limp strands around her neck. I took her hand and told her to come and sit next to me on the couch. She gave a soft moan that grew louder and louder until it was a shrill scream. She began to wail, yet for some reason I felt utterly tranquil. I knew without a doubt that an entity was attempting to come through her to speak. I wasn't frightened. Instead, I wanted to quiet my sister and get her to take charge of the situation.

"Gloria, sit down, calm down, and take control of your own body," I instructed her. "An entity—someone or something—is attempting to use your body and your vocal chords to speak through you. I've seen this happen before, but never spontaneously. Take your time. You have a choice. Only you can decide what will happen. Do you understand what I'm saying?"

"I'll be strangled if I let it speak. Help me! I'm scared," Gloria answered.

I remained composed. I stood up beside the couch and drew an imaginary line around my sister, calling on God to protect me and my sister and guide us through what was to come:

"Heavenly Father,

Encircle us with light and love.
Protect and guide us. Fill our minds, our
hearts, and our souls with only goodness. Let
no one enter unless they come from the light.
What is it that we must hear, and who is it
that wants to speak through Gloria's vocal
chords? Remember, oh, most gracious Virgin
Mary, that never was it known that anyone

who fled to thy protection, implored thy help, or sought thy intercession was left unaided.

Inspired by this confidence, I fly unto thee, oh Virgin of virgins, my mother; to thee do I come, before thee I stand, sinful and sorrowful. Oh Mother of the Word Incarnate, despise not my petitions, but, in thy mercy, hear and answer me, Amen."

The prayers of my youth came back to me as I prayed for strength, to know how to proceed with my sister. My words reassured Gloria; she tilted her eyes upward, and I could see that she was going to be alright.

I went into her bedroom, returned with a comfy white robe, and put it around her. The color came back into her cheeks and she tensed up as she leaned toward me, listening to something that I could not hear.

Her body began to twitch and the fingers of the lovely hands she had so often modeled inelegantly clawed the air. Her face glowed, but her eyes held a strange, faraway look. She yawned several times, then a woman's voice, different than Gloria's, came through her vocal cords, and she clutched the back of her neck as she uttered words in tones unlike her own. The voice said that over the next three days, Gloria would be given proof that she was in communication with beings of other consciousness and from other dimensions.

The woman emphasized that her message was simple. "My name is Maryha," she said. "And my message is that the course of human evolution lies in the ability of humans to love one another unconditionally. I am of the Light and come from a planet called Plutarm. I am here to assist you with your physical transformation. I will be close to you at all times."

Maryha spoke in monotone, "I live by unconditional love. Love is the essence of growth. Without giving and receiving love, the individual cannot grow in spirit."

Maryha gave personal messages to Gloria. She informed her that she would be leaving south Florida shortly. Gloria was saddened and refused to believe she would ever leave the tropical paradise she so loved. "Leave Florida, never!" was her retort. Maryha assured her that she would be moved for a greater purpose.

When the spontaneous channeling ended, Gloria's body returned to normal, but her face filled with horror. "What happened? Was I speaking? How can this be happening to me? Was another woman inside me? Am I possessed? Am I crazy? Oh Susan, am I losing my mind?" She sobbed hoarsely until she wore herself out and then continued to sniffle softly.

"Do crazy people know they're crazy?" I asked to get her to think more rationally. "Glo, haven't you ever seen anyone channel before? Have you heard of Lazurus (Jach Pursel); Seth (Jane Roberts); or Ramtha (J.Z. Knight)? They're all well-known channelers. You're not crazy, but why this is happening to you, I don't know. All I know is you shouldn't be afraid."

I was a bit spooked myself, but I tried not to let on to my sister. I even wondered if this was truly an otherworldly communication or some kind of psychosis.

Sheepishly, Gloria confided in me that while lying on the table during an earlier session with Dr. Shih, she had received a telepathic message that she would be subjected to a complete physical and psychological transformation, if she so agreed. She was given information regarding each step of the process and was told, "Beginning soon and for a three day period, your eyes shall change noticeably, both to you and those who know you. They shall turn from shades of the brown earth, to green as the seas, to blue like the flecks of color in marble. The freckles on your face will fade over time and dramatically disappear."

"I've been asking for proof that I'm not crazy, even before this happened today. The changes in my eyes will prove that I'm not nuts, that something truly has happened to me."

Overcome by exhaustion and hyperventilating from crying, Gloria stepped over to the glass doors just as the rain began to beat against the steel and concrete deck outside our apartment on the twenty-fourth floor of our high-rise on Treasure Island. As she closed the doors, the wind swirled the rain and the stormy weather rapped out a tattoo against the glass.

It was only ten a.m., but Gloria went into her bedroom and undressed slowly, hearing specific telepathic instructions from the female voice she had channeled. Frightened, she pulled the covers over her head and curled into a fetal position. She fell instantly asleep.

Mid-afternoon, I heard a strange noise coming from her bedroom. I opened the door to see my sister, still in the fetal position, sucking loudly on her thumb like a baby. Her body began to quiver, and her movements were uncoordinated. Whimpering and sucking, she bore down on the mattress, harder, faster, as if coming through the birth canal out into the open air. She screeched a newborn's cry as if just finding her breath. She was reliving her beginning, her "birth," but what I was witnessing was really her spontaneous re-birth.

Overwhelmed, she rose from the bed and slipped on a white cotton nightgown. For some reason, she prostrated herself like a Muslim Holy Man at Friday prayer. I thought she was in pain.

"Shut the blinds Susan, the light is burning my eyes," she told me.

Her alabaster face was framed by her dark, uncombed hair. The aftermath of the tropical storm sent sunlight streaming through the window.

"Shut the blinds Susan, the light is burning my eyes," she said again.

"Are you sick?" I asked her.

"No, I'm not sick. I've been light scanned. The information from the scanning device will be computed to determine the state of my physical health. It's a diagnostic tool much like those our doctors use, only far more advanced than any of our so-called 'state-of-the-art' equipment." Gloria spoke in an odd, robotic tone.

"Susan, the acupuncture opened me up as a channel and created a flow of enzymes throughout my body. Maryha explained the process by calling it Endocreosis[1]. A section of my liver has been cell-scraped and removed for testing. Fluid has been removed from my spine, in a procedure similar to a spinal tap. I've been told that I have a pre-chronic, disabling disorder of the liver which can be healed by a concentrated diet of calcium, protein and starch."

I was aghast at what I was hearing. "My God, Gloria! Who are these beings and what are they doing to you? Are they experimenting on you? What are you talking about? You don't sound like you, at all. This has gone too far."

Calmly, Gloria pointed to a large vein behind her right knee. I bent to inspect the blue line visible through her pale skin. The puncture mark there was unmistakable. Had someone pricked her with a needle?

"I am not sick; I'm going to be fine. I've been injected with a protein mixture and a vitamin pack," my sister told me.

I fell to the floor, stunned. Who had been here? Was this still my sister? What in God's name was going on here?

Gloria slumped onto the couch. Glancing over at her, I thought she looked small and vulnerable, like an infant. She began to suck her thumb intently, so I did the only thing a

---

[1]Endocreosis (the word) was channeled by Gloria and the spelling verified by Maryha when we could not find it in the dictionary. There is a word endocrinosis which refers to the hormone system in the body. However according to Maryha, endocreosis has a different meaning and describes a specific process.

mother could. I held her in my arms, cuddling the grown sister who was now acting like a baby.

My mind raced. What should I do? Minutes, and then an hour passed, my sister still unable to talk, still cuddled in my arms. Panic streaked across her baby face, and then she seemed to age into a toddler. The two sides of her brain formed words in juxtaposition but only a small child's words escaped, "Ma, ma, ma, ma-ma, Mama, Mommy. Da, da, da, Dad-dy. Da-a-a-dy." The toddler within her woman's body played with her hands and feet, exploring them.

Intermittently, Gloria ate and slept throughout the day. Her body craved adult food, but the small child within could not chew. This episode was bizarre, but I was determined to get her through it—whatever "it" was. I was terrified but didn't want to leave her alone to go for help. For some insane reason, it never occurred to me that I should call Dr. Shih.

I made tapioca pudding and fed it to her. My sister was peaceful now, as though she had fully entrusted herself to the care of a higher consciousness.

The second day followed the same pattern. I was the caretaker, and Gloria, the child. Instructions were given to her telepathically and she relayed each message in the singsong tones of a child. I obeyed whatever she told me to do. Every few hours, I was told to increase the calcium and protein level of her food. Before long, she was able to eat solid food if I cut it up for her.

On the third day, she appeared to be more like an adult, and the ability to speak like one had returned. "Susan, go run your errands; it's okay," she told me. "You can leave. I'm feeling normal again."

I wasn't so sure I should leave Gloria alone. However, I went out because I needed to. I took a drive and tried to collect my thoughts. I felt I should take some responsibility and call a doctor. But...what kind of doctor—a psychiatrist? Or should I call a priest?

I located a phone booth on Miami Beach and decided to call my sister, Ananfaye. She lived in Mt. Shasta and was known as a healer. She was well-versed in paranormal phenomena, though I had never heard her mention anything like this. She'd had her own Kundalini experience at the Pyramids of Giza, Egypt, a few years prior. She believed that the incident had opened her spiritually. Kundalini (taken from yoga) is seen as an energy that lies dormant at the base of the spine. When this energy is awakened, it rises slowly up the spine to the top of the head. The idea is that the Kundalini energy removes all blocks and awakens consciousness as it moves upward. It is purification or a balancing of the body. Often, it leads to a spiritual awakening to one's true path. As I stood beside the phone booth, I suddenly couldn't bring myself to dial Ananfaye's number.

Defeated, I went back home. Maybe I, too, had gone mad. I was allowing the drama to continue—but could I really stop it?

Gloria stood in front of a mirror in the hall examining her eyes as I walked in. I watched from behind her as sunlight filtered across the mirror. The outer circumference of one iris had turned a shade of blue. The color circled halfway around it.

"They're actually changing color, just like they told me," she said.

Impossible! It couldn't be, but I looked more closely and her eye was still brown around the pupil, but the outer edge of the iris was definitely blue.

"Look Susan, I *am* different! My eyes aren't the same. This is proof of what's happening, just like I was told." Gloria smiled at herself in the mirror, and I froze in place for a few seconds, my mind reeling from the events of the last three days.

I looked at her again and said, "My God! Not only are your eyes changing color, but your retina has changed shape.

Your eyes are rounder, wider in the center and tapering outward in a slight slant."

I walked over to the bookshelf and picked up one of my sister's professional modeling portfolios. On the second page, an indoor color headshot carefully staged by the photographer revealed a young woman with intense brown eyes. I thumbed through the pages and saw clearly that Gloria's eyes had never held even a hint of the almond shape now so visible. Every picture showed a smiling, brown-eyed girl. A chill ran down my spine and I took a deep breath.

On the third day, Gloria was informed by Maryha that her physical transformation was complete. She stood in the sunlight clutching her wooly, stuffed animal named "Lamb Chops" in her hand. Her narrow body seemed childlike through the white cotton of her gown, but the deep red nipples and dark pubic hair that could be seen through her nightgown identified her as a woman.

My little sister spoke in a barely audible voice, "I have completed my transition. I have made an agreement. I have been told of many planetary events to come which I have not relayed to you. I am a messenger of the light. I am a link in the chain that connects others to their paths of light. You are to know dear sister that as I channel this information through me as it is also for you. You have been called as a spiritual counselor to run the light of God into dense areas and where darkness has settled. You will thus be known as a Lightrunner™.

All the links I connect will form a stronger bond for change. Those who hear me will know that my message rings true. My information comes from a higher energy whose source is derived from the light of God."

"An agreement, what do you mean? With whom?" I asked.

"I have agreed to become a human receiver and have allowed these beings from Plutarm to study my body. My messages are received by way of a micro-chip transmitter that has been placed in the lower left lobe of my cerebral area. It is so state of the art that earthly ultra sound instruments cannot detect the presence of the chip that has been placed in my head."

"Sister, I need to know that you accept my choice. I feel the truth within me. I am still your little sister, Gloria, but I am changed. I am still the Gloria who wants children, a family and a home, all that I have longed for but have never seemed to gain. I am of the earth, but I belong to the universe. Love me just as you have in the past. I love you."

I tried to lighten up the conversation and turned to Gloria to show her my new peridot earrings, which I had purchased since I had read that "peridot" wards off evil.

Gloria did not seem to be listening but had two fingers pressed against her temple. "Turn up the volume," she said loudly to Maryha.

"Are the hanging objects on your sister's ears mechanically important? Why do you hang things on your ears? The practice is most interesting. Is it to signal to 'receive from one another?'"

Gloria burst into laughter. "I guess we are just as different to Maryha as she is to us?"

The somber mood was broken.

Maryha was all around, monitoring thoughts, observing actions and listening to conversations. It was creepy.

Gloria yelled out, "The E.T. is signaling me." She was immediately corrected by a gentle transmission from Maryha who informed her that she was not an E.T., nor an alien, but that she was a galactic being.

Maryha had no sense of humor.

Maryha said that "our work will separate and reunite us but that our work would be closely aligned with one another throughout our lives."

"You and your sister shall be known as Lightrunners."

"Lightrunner," Gloria broke off the transmission. "What does Maryha mean? I need money. Does the job pay?" Do I need a job with a boss from another planet? Running the Light?

Lightrunner, a messenger, a running light, navigation, aviation; the word had many meanings.

Gloria mused, "Lightrunner, I am as of today a Lightrunner."

Susan, "You are a Lightrunner and your work has already begun. We are to be called Lightrunners."

Chapter 13
1989 — Encounter

On the Tuesday that I had decided to tell Carlos that I didn't love him and end the relationship, it happened. I had an encounter.

At dusk, the last of the fireball sun dipped below the city's skyline. Glancing toward the night sky, I turned off the air conditioning and opened the doors to the balcony of my 24th floor apartment. Stepping outside, I looked down. All I could see was the water and a tiny strip of land leading to the dock below. The angle of the building lent itself to a dramatic view not only of a strip of the coastal waterway but also of the Miami skyline abutting the endless Atlantic Ocean. Gloria and Lance had found the apartment and the three of us had leased it for the view.

The expanse of glass doors that opened onto the balcony from every room made me feel as though I lived among the stars. Every time I stood out there, the same thought occurred to me, *an artist should live here—a painter—not me*. I glanced up into the ebony sky, unable to tell where the water ended and the night began. I heard the waves far below, and the sound mesmerized me. The night was partly cloudy, obscuring the stars, but through the telescope I kept on the patio, I could identify the Big Dipper and Orion, and I could see Pleiades to the north.

Later, I slipped off my clothes and lay down on the bed in hopes of getting a good night's sleep. I had talked at length on the phone to my sister in California where it was three hours earlier, and because it wasn't late for her, I'd lost track of time. The bedside clock read 12:45 a.m. I put a cassette on the tape recorder and closed my eyes to listen to the music and the ocean sounds.

The combination soothed away the day's fatigue that permeated my body. I began to relax and enjoy the feel of the balmy breeze against my skin. I stretched out flat on my back. Slowly, I let my muscles go limp. I drowsed and drifted into a hypno-gogic state of bliss—until I attempted to flip over onto my stomach and found I could not.

I grew instantly alert when I realized my body wouldn't obey the commands of my brain. My muscles felt paralyzed. I tried to lift an arm up and push myself up on the bed. The arm wouldn't budge. I took a deep breath and tried again. Maybe my arm had fallen asleep. But no, there was no numbness, yet my arm held fast as if superglued to the bedcovers. My head pounded with my elevated blood pressure. I felt like I was about to have a stroke, or worse.

"What's wrong with me? Why can't I move?" I asked aloud.

I moved only when the telepathic command seared my brain. I stood beside the bed and thought about turning off the music but my hand wouldn't allow me the choice. Unaware that I was still naked, I walked to the open door leading to the balcony and stepped out onto the cool cement. I leaned against the wrought iron railing of the ledge and looked out at the spectacular view. Light crystals dotted the blackness. Was it a series of stars? As I watched, it seemed as though the lights moved closer.

Abruptly, I straightened and looked directly upward. A thin laser of blue-white light maneuvered toward me, striking my right eye just beside my pupil. The flash stung my iris, and I blinked wildly. I felt as though a needle had pierced my eye socket. I covered my eye with my hand and the pain immediately stopped. The light beam widened and a strange odor permeated the sultry air. I had no idea why I had come outdoors.

My heart pounded with fear. Disoriented, I glanced through the glass back into the bedroom to view my empty bed, and as I did so, I was surrounded by an intense white light. I began to sweat profusely as I breathed in the peculiar odor that surrounded me. Chills ran the length of my spine.

Alarmed, I peered into the light trying to find its source. The crystal dots I had seen earlier rapidly transformed into a series of orbs of multi-colored lights that pulsated around a disc-shaped object. I watched it hover over my building, and I estimated that it was at least 50-75 feet in diameter. The craft was shiny in color, like solid hematite. It emitted no sound, not even a hum. It wasn't an airplane, and it was larger than a helicopter. Not even the slightest breeze was stirred as the object lingered in the sky.

"It's a spaceship. Holy Jesus, that's what it is!" I breathed.

Before I was lifted into the starless sky, I saw an amber glow encircled by beams of blue-white light.

"Oh, dear God, they're taking me with them!" I cried out to the night. As I was lifted into the air, a beam of light kept me warm even though my body was bare and I knew the temperature should be growing colder as I gained altitude.

I felt embarrassed to be floating naked in space above the building, thinking I could be seen from below. I was suspended horizontally in the darkness, arms frozen at my sides, face down. People walked toward the dock on the narrow pavement, but nobody glanced up at me. If they had, I would have been invisible to them. Then my body angled into a vertical position, and I shot upward like a rocket launched into space.

I ascended through an opening in the craft into a room brilliant with light, expecting to find that I had awakened to the radiant morning sun. Instead, I was in a circular room lined with honeycombed panels that stretched from the floor to rounded ceiling.

Coming out of my trance-like state, I realized that the multiple rows I was seeing weren't honeycombs but soft fabric slots designed to look like them. The small openings in the pale yellow crevices were filled with tiny tools and larger instruments, several tuning forks, pieces of quartz in various sizes, and clear pouch-like containers filled with a finely ground, green powdered substance that looked like Japanese *matcha* tea.

There was no sound in the room, nor was there anyone in sight. I saw no furniture of any kind. I couldn't fathom where I had entered the craft because there were no visible doors or windows. An instrument panel, many times larger than any I had ever seen in the cockpit of an airplane, dominated one wall. Huge celestial navigation charts, bigger than any found on the bridge of a cruise ship, filled another entire wall. A third wall was taken up with what looked like a series of computer monitors alight with undecipherable symbols.

I surmised that the atmosphere was a censoring device that scanned my physical being as well as my thoughts and emotions because whenever I moved or took a deep breath, or thought, "What's going on?" the monitors would light up and record new symbols. Although I couldn't read the symbols, their formations reminded me of the crop circles I'd seen in an English magazine. If I moved or bent my body, the atmosphere around me took in the data and coded the symbols relative to my body parts as my physiology appeared on the screen.

I knew I was correct as to the monitoring of my body and emotions, not because I completely understood what was going on, but because the information was being transmitted to me telepathically in cryptic forms, stilted word taps that sounded like auditory Morse code. "You—are—correct, we—are—monitoring—your—physical—welfare—and—thoughts." Tap—tap—tap: the tele-thoughts were transferred from some unknown being to me.

The only discomfort I felt was the odd sensation in my numb, frozen body. My eye still throbbed slightly, but there was no pain. The terror I had first felt was being replaced by fascination as I hung in suspended animation and took in the room around me.

I looked up at the dome-like ceiling and realized that the large room had been molded together without seams or any visible source of light. Yet the room was over bright, and I had to periodically shut my eyes or blink rapidly to adjust them. Waves of light altered the color in the room. At first glimpse, it was bright white, but as I became accustomed to it, I detected iridescent pearl and shades of gray alloy.

Without a sound, a being materialized in front of me. Even though I saw no physical attributes upon which to base my decision—no breasts, no defining curves—I felt certain that the creature was female. She exuded a feminine charisma. She was over six feet tall and green in color, thin and lithe, like a ballerina. Her eyes were liquid, dark green and inky black, like chiseled glass, the color of *moldovite* (a greenish crystal known for its healing qualities), almond-shaped and too large for her face. They tapered in slants to the sides of her face. She had no eyelids or eyebrows. Her large, bulbous cranium was hairless, too. She had no ears, and her tiny nostrils lay flat on her face; there was no bone or cartilage. The creature's mouth was lipless, only a thin slit with no tongue or saliva visible.

Her body appeared pliable as though molded from clay. I couldn't tell if she wore clothes. It was as if a layer of protective outer garments molded to her body gave the effect of a vinyl jumpsuit. Her hands were graceful. She had four fingers and a thumb as long as the other fingers. The fingers were close together creating a webbed effect. She had no fingernails, nothing extraneous. She had a long, elegant neck, which turned slowly on its axis. She could rotate it completely around from front to back and side-to-side. I was still a bit frightened, but my curiosity took over, and I couldn't stop staring at her.

The creature transferred her thoughts to me but spoke no words from her mouth. She answered my questions as soon as they formed in my mind. She communicated with me, but I couldn't fully understand what she was saying. I understood only bits of the "conversation." The rest seemed to be garbled syllables of unfamiliar syntax. Her telepathic thought transfers were terse and unfamiliar, and single words resounded in clipped timbre as if breaking up over a wireless transmission. I strained to hear the foreign combination of sound and telepathy. Mostly she used what I thought was a technique of scanning my mind.

I gleaned from the distorted communication that a colleague was coming into the room and that I was going to be chronicled by the two of them. A panel dropped down from the wall into the space in front of me. It was made of a shiny metal-like material and had six legs. It was as thin as a massage table and weightless. A mechanical device unfolded from the wall and spread a gray substance over the table. I was directed to climb onto it and lie flat on my back. When I did so, I found that gray substance had the consistency of cotton candy and cushioned my body.

Particles of light rearranged themselves before my eyes and another creature like the female presented himself to me. He, too, had no visible sexual organs, but I identified him by his male energy. He seemed very serious, but the female appeared to assert more authority. He signaled to her as she leaned over me to take my hand and position it over my right eye. She moved my hand back and forth several times over my eye and liquid drops moistened the surface. The drops appeared to come from the rapid movement of the woman's webbed hands over mine; however, the moisture originated in my own hand. The throbbing and stinging that had resurfaced in my eye ceased immediately.

The man gave silent commands gesturing to the instrument panel and/or the honeycomb wall with his hands. I watched carefully, trying to comprehend. As he signaled, an instrument would appear from the shelf of the compartment and he would guide it toward me without actually touching me. The instruments from different compartments changed quickly: a tiny knife came first to scrape the nape of my neck; a long tool with a clamp-like device on the end checked inside my nostrils; and a skinny shovel scooped skin from behind my left knee before he completed more intrusive procedures.

He performed a pelvic exam with a cold object, and he scraped tissue from my cervix. I couldn't tell whether he used his hand or another instrument to do this; I only knew that it was freezing cold, and it should have hurt, but it didn't. The probing continued. After each procedure, his female colleague would take the material collected, insert it into one of the clear pouches filled with fluid, and hold it against the monitor to record the data for analysis. He motioned again, and two long needles appeared. He stuck a needle in each of my ears and placed several more along the soles of my feet. My feet tingled and balls of blue light emitted from them. I felt a slight electrical current jolt through my body.

The female creature touched me, and I understood that the pain would subside soon. I felt caressed, and unmistakably, I heard her say in tap mode, "You—have—no—pain.—Your—pain—is—gone.—You—cannot—feel—any—pain.—Your—body—is—calm.—There—is—no—pain.—You—cannot—feel—pain." As soon as I heard her words, I felt no pain, only the tingling.

Blood, warm and glutinous, seeped from my nostrils. She touched the bridge of my nose, and the bleeding stopped. I smelled unfamiliar ethers. I watched the monitors on the wall as they registered each command and the screen blinked and flashed in an assortment of colors.

The outlandish scene seemed familiar. It somehow reminded me of an autopsy I'd watched on television. The TV doctor examined each organ as he cut it out, audibly discussing its condition as he dissected the body. There was the same critical analysis of my parts, but I was alive and fully conscious, and there was no visible cutting. The creature/doctor/scientist silently transferred data to the computer with a shift of his hand in some form of silent communication.

I lay still, not uncomfortable, but suspended in time. I was unable to move of my own volition. I couldn't tell if I'd been there for a short while or if it had been several hours. My concept of time had vanished into the present moment. Awareness was temporary.

All the while, the two otherworldly colleagues communicated in perfect harmony. As he continued the probe, the male doctor would hesitate and wait for the female to place my hand over the area he had just worked on before he moved to the next area of my body. She seemed to be assisting me to heal by using my own body energy.

The female stared at me and I heard, "The—probe—is—over.—Stay—on—the—table—for—a—few—moments—and—you—will—feel—better.—We—are—finished—here.–You—will—feel—normal—tomorrow.—I—will—hear—you—if—you—need—me—or—are—in—any—pain.—I—will—tell—you—what—to—do.—If—you—need—me— please—ask—for—me."

The woman took a layered blanket of pale yellow gauze and laid it over my nude body as I recovered from the ordeal. Then she took a snake-shaped bottle and misted me with a liquid that soothed me. Kindly, as if she was a mother feeding her child, the creature took a clear bag from one of the compartments and directed me to take a portion of the green powder within it between my fingers. I took a miniscule portion of the green powder, and she opened my mouth. I sprinkled the powder onto my tongue and swallowed the chalky substance. Then I sat up easily, already beginning to feel better. I let the blanket slip to one side. She picked it up, and a mechanical arm extended from the wall, took the gauzy blanket and folded it before placing it in one of the smaller honeycombed compartments.

Both beings busied themselves as I stretched to allow my limbs to return to their usual dexterity. I could see that the doctor beings were engrossed with the images on the monitors. Minute samples of my bodily tissues had been placed in the pouches with the clear fluid. As the male doctor held up each sample in front of the monitor, lights blinked and data from the sample's silhouette was recorded. After a long silence, the two doctors left the room just as eerily as they had appeared.

Feeling physically quite normal, I moved freely as I peered about the room. There were other beings gathered in another room behind the wall. I couldn't see them, but I knew that room was where the creatures had gone, and that they were discussing me with others. I decided to explore. I crossed the space toward the shiny panels, pushing and probing each panel, convinced one would be a door. I touched a slightly irregular panel and it fell open.

I put my right foot through the narrow aperture that looked more like a window than a door, expecting to see the room where the others had gathered. Instead, I glanced down to see my foot as it sank into the rose-tinted carpet in my Miami apartment. I was cold and tired and I shivered in my nakedness. I looked at the clock on the wall; it was 3:45 a.m. My right eye was tearing up, and my legs and arms ached as though I'd been lifting heavy weights.

Shock numbed my freezing body as I walked into the bedroom and flicked on the light. Moving to the dresser, I pulled out a drawer looking for a nightgown or T-shirt that would warm me. I caught my reflection in the mirror above the dresser and was startled to see that my eyes were red and irritated. I looked hung-over, sick. My skin was ashen. My stomach throbbed, and I glanced down at my flat abdomen. Across its surface were three dark, reddish-blue, round marks, each slightly larger than a silver dollar. I stood before the mirror and examined them. Strange—I didn't remember the creatures doing anything to my stomach. Seeing the marks recalled a roundup on a ranch in Montana, the year I visited a friend and watched her uncle brand a small calf when I was ten.

I slipped a cotton shift over my head thinking I would call Dr. Shih tomorrow and have her take a look at the strange circles. I fell into a deep sleep and slept until the heat from the open doors seeped in early the next afternoon. I awoke overheated and reached down to pull off my white sleeveless gown. My face was warm, and I swiped a hand across my forehead. I sat up and red drops fell from my nose. I took the shift and blotted my bleeding nose.

I remembered the marks and glanced at my stomach. The symmetry of the circles looked ludicrous in the sunlight. *How am I going to wear a bikini?* I wondered. *I'm a mess. How did I get these blue bruises?* I looked down at my slim legs and saw nothing amiss. *Thank God! Oh, I suppose, these marks will heal,* I told myself.

I walked over to the telephone and dialed my boyfriend's number. "Carlos, I slept in late this morning. Do we still have time to go to the beach today while you're off? Can you meet me?"

"Baby, I let you sleep in because I was exhausted myself from traveling. I spent the morning doing paperwork and drinking coffee. The beach sounds terrific. Meet you at 2:00 by the large palm, our usual place, before the wind comes up?"

I responded, "I'll be there, sweetie." I dropped the phone onto its cradle. Then I took a scalding shower and dried myself slowly, on the lookout in case I found any more unwanted surprises. I pulled on a one-piece bathing suit, picked up my favorite beach towel and some soft blankets, and walked the twenty-four floors down to the street level.

I strolled down the boulevard to meet Carlos. He was waiting at our spot when I arrived. I smiled when I saw his wonderful face. I forgot the night's ordeal and wanted to believe I'd dreamed up the whole incident. I felt the burn marks as I touched my stomach. No, I wasn't getting off that easy—something otherworldly had truly happened.

After a splash in the waves, we lazed the afternoon away. The beach was empty. I snuggled up to Carlos until I felt his organ rise. He guided my hand downward and pulled the beach towel over us as we hollowed out the damp sand. I lifted soft blankets from my beach bag and spread them over the towel. Underneath our coverings, I stroked him gently at first, then faster, harder and faster, until he came all over my leg and semen dripped into the nest we'd made in the sand. He groaned and squeezed me to him. He relaxed and smiled at me when I took my sticky hand, drew it up to my mouth and licked my fingers. He clutched me tighter and kissed me softly on the mouth. Carlos loved me with all his heart, and I knew it.

We dozed in the fading sun until the wind came in from the sea signaling the end of our beach day. We packed up our beach togs and walked to his apartment. It was smaller than mine, but we both liked its sunny colors and intimate style. Carlos fixed a light supper of *ceviche* (a Cuban or South American dish of raw marinated fish in citrus juices) and black bean soup with hot Cuban bread. I showered alone while he made dinner, then wrapped myself in a new *pareu* (a Tahitian sarong), and lit candles, placing them on the nightstand before turning out all the lights. We ate and drank wine, sitting out on the patio until midnight. We fell into bed laughing over the stories Carlos told me of his travels.

In the dark, he never noticed the spots on my stomach; he was too busy kissing me elsewhere. The spots hadn't begun to scab and he moved his hands across my tummy without feeling anything amiss. He held me close to him in bed, sensing my usual detachment.

"Susan, marry me," he urged.

I kissed him on the mouth and snuggled my face into his hairy chest. I sucked his erect nipples one at a time then moved my mouth downward, circling his belly and moving closer to his groin. As I nibbled and nuzzled downward, he forgot what he had asked, and I was too otherwise occupied to comment.

Later, in my sleep, I screamed out, "No, no! Let me go!" Carlos said I sounded terrified, but he held me to him, and I slept soundly the rest of the night cradled in his arms.

It was days before I realized that I had told no one about the abduction. Not even Carlos. Had this been an encounter of the fourth kind? Had I skipped over or forgotten the second and third encounters, since the first one happened so long ago?

Several weeks later, I told Carlos that I wanted the relationship to end. It took time to process the events of the abduction, and the comfort of being with him caused me to delay ending the relationship. (Great sex is a powerful antidote, so I clung to him both emotionally and sexually awhile longer to soothe the torment of my experience).

He was hurt and angry with me and left for Puerto Rico the next day. I called his family's compound in Puerto Rico. He wouldn't speak to me. Never before had a man refused to maintain communication with me after the breakup. Most of my relationships ended on friendly terms, and some remained intimate. Both husbands and I made love for a period of time after I divorced them, and I knew I could always count on them for anything and vice-versa. But I never saw or heard from Carlos again.

My sister Gloria had moved to New York, and the morning after my brush with aliens, my new roommate said, "I got up early this morning to get a glass of water, and there you were lying nude beside the window on the rose carpet talking to some 'beings' in a language I couldn't make heads or tails of. I went back into my bedroom, and the creatures left. Later, you seemed completely normal. You went and got your robe and came out into the living room for coffee." My friend and roommate was an extraordinary person, a well-known astrologer and psychic from San Francisco named Eloise, who had lived an incredulous life of her own. My encounter with aliens was nothing out of the ordinary to her way of thinking, as I found out that day. That's why she went back to her room and didn't interrupt, and that's why she was so blasé when she later mentioned what she'd seen to me.

Chapter 14
1990 – Call to Service

It took me years to discover the overlay of grief my mother's suicide created within me just as it forever altered my worldview. The fact that I was intuitive yet had not been able to see what she was planning undermined me. "Impossible," is what I would have said had anyone dared to suggest that my devout Catholic mother would ever have killed herself, depressed or not. The word "possible" in this case never crossed my mind. Mother never threatened to kill herself, or mentioned the word "suicide," or said that she wanted to die; she wrote no suicide note. My siblings and I were left to deal with our own guilt for not deciphering the clues she may have been trying to give us. Her suicide, coupled with my abduction experience, tore down any mental fences I may have created due to society's standards, and I had to accept all possibilities as valid. I realized that the word "impossible" was relative. Nothing was impossible now.

I felt violated by the abduction and the subsequent probe that had occurred while I was aboard the craft. The round burn spots on my stomach, now faint and light, still reminded me of the encounter. I had stepped over the edge, and I could not go back. I was like a "fringe dweller," the term used to describe the Aborigines I'd seen in Australia, those people who were displaced and living on the edges outside the cities. The government had taken the children from their families in the bush and forced them into the white man's world by placing them in their boarding schools. When the mandates of that society changed, they were released and had to live "betwixt and between," unable to return to their past life in the bush or to fully assimilate into urban culture. They were outcasts who hung around where they weren't wanted.

I felt the same way.

My sister's experience—which I had shared in by caretaking her—along with my own alien encounter, was by design a "meaningful coincidence" in the Jungian sense— synchronistic. Too many unlikely occurrences had brought us together in Miami and conspired to change our paths.

I began to reconstruct my life into two parts: before the encounter and after the encounter.

The alien woman who had examined me in the spacecraft became a constant presence in my life. Clearly, she was not Maryha, who Gloria channeled. She never actually gave me her name. Maybe she didn't have one. Nor do I think I ever asked. In retrospect, I find it quite unusual that I did not connect a name with her or wonder where she had come from. I simply accepted her presence.

She telepathically contacted me, advising me what foods to buy, to cook, and to eat. She insisted I re-examine my health, which at the time seemed perfect. I barely listened as she gave advice on calorie limits and foods that would improve my well-being.

As I wandered the market at Wild Oats or Unicorn Village in Miami, I heard, "Buy kale and spinach; up your calcium and potassium. Consume more water; filter your water. Eat only organic products without preservatives or pesticides. Don't eat the meat of any animal that has been raised with hormones in its feed. Eat chicken livers."

Chicken livers? I thought they were high in cholesterol, I argued back telepathically.

"Watch the mercury content in the fish you are buying." How in this world was I supposed to check the mercury count in the fish I bought?

She said to recycle everything, and to conserve water. The creature constantly reminded me that our resources are limited, and that each individual must conserve and recycle or planet Earth would be depleted of its resources.

In the beginning, the information she gave me was fascinating, but before long, I got bored with her advice since it only related to my health, and I felt there was nothing wrong with me. I stopped listening and months later, the transmissions slowed and her sermons eventually stopped. I would have been wise to heed the lectures.

At the time, it was much more interesting to me to understand how I was able to receive her telepathic transmissions. I knew I was an empath and that I received psychic imprints from others here on earth, or deceased, but how was I able to receive data from aliens, or was it a galactic being?

Had they done a brain scan using an MRI (magnetic resonance imaging) or PET (positron emission tomography)? Was that what now enabled me to "hear" my alien "mentor"?

A PET scan is created by injecting radioactive sugar into the subject's bloodstream. The sugar activates the portions of the brain that utilize the thinking process. The radioactive sugar releases positrons (anti-electrons) that are easily identified by special instruments. By tracing the path of the anti-matter in the living brain, thought patterns can be discerned, and it can be determined what parts of the brain are engaged in a given activity.

The MRI machine operates in a similar manner. The subject's head is placed in a magnetic field that causes the nuclei of the atoms in the brain to align with those in the field. A radio pulse is sent into the nuclei and causes them to vibrate.

Alternatively, was there some other force that accounted for this telepathy—apart from gravity, electromagnetism, or the nuclear forces, both weak and strong? Weak nuclear forces come from radioactive decay and strong nuclear forces hold the center of the atom together. The energy of the sun and stars originates from nuclear forces. Could this fifth source of telepathy be a "psi" force?

Some physicists, like the visionary Michio Kaku, say it is likely.

Is it possible to use simple Newtonian and Maxwellian physics to explain telepathy via radio? The brain *is* a transmitter through which our thoughts are sent out in the form of tiny electrical signals and electromagnetic waves, but the signals are too weak for us to be able to read another's thoughts; likely in the milliwatt range. Does this mean it is impossible?

Only crude information about our thoughts have been currently collected, since the signals are scrambled, or gibberish. We have no known antennae, so how can we receive messages sent from other brains? Such telepathy seems impossible for humans but appears to have been mastered by other species in the galaxy.

These phenomena puzzled me. I tried to learn as much as I could about the subject because I thought that the transmissions I first received were oral, and spoken in abrupt tones or gibberish, especially while I was aboard the craft.

Whenever I now receive such information during a client reading, it comes from collective sources, which I simply refer to as Spirit. The messages come from deceased relatives, spirit guides—both mine and theirs—angelic beings, alien species and other living beings. I hear specific words sometimes in foreign languages. I see silent videos that I must interpret. I "know" things in a kinesthetic sense, feel things that have happened to the recipient of the reading in the past, and I can clearly see their future. If an entity attempts to enter my body—usually through the back of my neck—use my vocal chords and change my voice to channel information, or wants to enter my body and contort my limbs, I don't allow it. That's why I always ask to receive the information telepathically when I am given a message for myself or for others.

My sister Gloria's psycho-spiritual crisis and physical transformation over the three-day period in Miami resulted in an uncannily accurate psychic ability. Always intuitive, she now honed her random psychic visions into skilled predictions when she did readings and group sessions. In these, she channeled an entity called "Maryha" who claimed to be from the planet Plutarm. When she first started doing this, Gloria tended to predict disasters—something that is difficult for the channel to deal with since knowing ahead of time about such things creates great anxiety.

I recall that she told me that there would be a severe earthquake, and that she saw small-boned, dark-skinned people running and trying to free themselves from the rubble. She thought it was to happen in the Pacific islands somewhere. When the quake struck the Philippines shortly thereafter in July 1990, she wondered why she had been forewarned of it; what could she have done?

Some of the information she received for herself was amazing. While living in Miami, she received a message from our deceased father who told her she would marry a doctor and be happy, that she would finally have the children she had always wanted. My other sisters and I got a chuckle out of that because what father with five daughters doesn't hope at least one of his daughters will marry a doctor or a lawyer?

Shortly after Gloria left Miami and moved to New York, she became a flight attendant for Pan Am Airlines. She had a flight to Los Angeles, and her attendant roommate invited her to join her and her brother for dinner there. He was both a doctor and a lawyer, and he could afford to take them somewhere fancy. Gloria agreed. It wasn't long after the two met in L.A. that they fell in love. Now, they are married and have two children.

After going through those three days with Gloria, my mother's suicide seemed normal compared to the seeming absurdity of an alien abduction, but that was before I experienced one myself. Gloria's physio-Kundalini experience allowed me to witness the amazing channeling experience of spontaneous movements, shifting body sensations and throat agitation. Because of this, I now questioned all preconceived notions of time and space, of what might or might not be true. I had to construct new ways of thinking about the extraordinary experiences I'd been part of.

While she was still in Miami, Gloria sought counsel. Dr. Brian Weiss (the celebrated psychiatrist who wrote *Many Masters, Many Lives)* had an office there. Liza James, one of his therapists, helped her deal with the continuing incidents of spontaneous channeling and the psychic visions that now permeated her waking moments.

Gloria poured out her fears to Liza, telling her, "I'm not a 'New Age' yuppie or a wannabe psychic—what's happening to me? Liza, can you help me? I need to be able to hold down a job and earn some money. Why is this happening to me now?

"At odd moments, especially when I meet someone new, I receive information about that person. If I speak to them momentarily, pass my hand across their handwriting, or hold an object they have touched, I know things about them, and I can see their past, present and future. This is frightening. It feels like too much responsibility. It's not me who knows all this, but it's Maryha, speaking through me. Am I making any sense?"

"You see," she continued, Maryha's the entity who helped me through my physical transformation. Maryha says that she monitors human thought patterns. This is not psychic predictions in her terminology, but scientific probabilities based on information contained in the individual's thought patterns.

"Liza, tell me you understand! Maryha has the ability to predict human behavior and she conveys it to me telepathically. Projection, Maryha says, is a scientific skill similar to our ability to analyze trends in economics, science and health." Gloria inhaled deeply as she told her story, afraid as she did so that the therapist might terminate the session and pronounce her "insane."

"Maryha's knowledge is computed from research annals. She says her memory bank is a hundred times greater than a humanoid's. I suddenly find myself knowledgeable about the human body and medicine. Maryha tells me that Western medicine is quite limited. Medical diagnosis is my forte. I can focus on a person's body and locate a diseased organ or a potential medical problem by a method of 'light scanning,' and if I touch the person's body, my hand immediately locates the diseased area.

"The medical terminology and the images produced in my brain are always unfamiliar to me, and I stumble through pronunciation. I have no medical background. Tell me Liza; am I crazy?"

The young therapist was skilled in her profession. Her many credentials hung in black frames behind her desk. She was familiar with the techniques of traditional psychotherapy. She was also skilled in non-traditional avenues such as hypnosis, a means by which a therapist could access the inner workings of the mind. Liza did what any good therapist should do. She didn't judge, but instead patiently led my sister to integrate the experience into her psyche and accept the fact that she—like her sister—was a medium. Liza helped her. That's all that mattered to me, so I didn't ask her much about the sessions or the hypnosis.

Still the question haunted me: What my sister and I experienced separately in Miami—was it real?

Once I had experienced what I perceived to be a UFO encounter of the fourth kind, my separation from the mainstream was complete. The loss of former friends and my peer group during my first divorce, my psychic abilities, my return to school, the loss of contact with my lover, and living away from my children after my second divorce had all worked to disconnect me from the friendships I'd known only as a wife, mother and homemaker living the good life in suburbia.

For several years, I lived along the margin, not belonging, feeling apart and actually suffering exclusion by my previous sets of friends. It was like living in an underworld, where normal cultural behavioral cues no longer worked. The inner journey my soul was leading me on meant I had to face certain truths about myself, including the fact that I had chosen two divorces; I had moved cross-country to flee my former life (but, in retrospect, I was actually running toward a new life); I had chosen to be alone, without a partner; and I was responsible for the erratic course of my law school journey. When I looked at the choices I had made thus far, I felt like I had entered the place within me that I called the *Dark Night of My Soul*. I identified with the words of St. John of the Cross he related in his writings as I fell into a place within that I had never been.

As Spirit is prone to do when you're not following your bliss, it shakes you to the core so that you are forced to reassess your priorities. The timing of my mother's suicide affected the very nucleus of my existence. My father's death at the beginning of law school and my mother's suicide shortly thereafter while I was still in law school, somewhat obliterated my choices concerning law school and the practice of law and forever changed the course of my journey. The money issues, the sadness, the inability to cope with the suicide and the single parenting of my teenagers (since their father was still drinking) took its toll upon me. I felt that the only help I had was from my parents and they were gone.

I was being called to something, and it was not the law. Every time I tried to continue on the course of becoming an attorney, I was thwarted by an outside force and had to re-group and revamp my expectations.

Certainly, the quickest way to alter a belief is by experiential learning. In Miami, my UFO encounter made my mother's suicide and my psychic abilities seem much less strange by comparison. When I altered one side of the equation, I had to alter the other. I knew the physical reality of the UFO encounter to be true because of the brands on my stomach and the pinpricks behind my knee. Mentally, the idea that I had been abducted and taken aboard a spaceship took time to accept. One piece of the "formula" can't exist without the other, and, because I had the physical proof, I gradually stopped calling my abduction "alleged."

In legal terms, *prima facie* evidence is "evidence having such a degree of probability that it must prevail unless the contrary be proved." I let go of my skepticism when I studied the scientific investigations and literature reviews of experts in the field. Slowly, I came to terms with what had happened to me and I believed.

The work of John E. Mack, M.D., Pulitzer Prize winner and Harvard psychiatrist, who wrote *Abduction, Human Encounters with Aliens*, detailing his work with abductees and recounting their experiences, told me that I was not alone.

I fell into a dark period of anxiety and extreme psychic impressions. Psychic visions are attunements to realms that we cannot detect with our five senses, presenting possible and probable outcomes. An increase in psychic sensitivity is one of the signs of spiritual awakening. It seemed to me that I had already opened to Spirit during the time of my painful divorce from my first husband. The existential crisis filled me with aberrant, reoccurring psychic flashes that caused insomnia at night and nervous edginess during the day. Was this a repeat? Had I not heeded the call the first time around?

I needed to earn money, so I began to read out of a metaphysical bookstore called "Whispers," in North Miami. I also read at fairs and large charity events. My sister, Ananfaye, the healer and astrologer, and I often talked about our spiritual journeys and our metaphysical musings. She asked me one day, "Why don't you do readings for serious money?"

And so I did.

I hung my shingle first outside an office on Miami Beach that I shared with a therapist and eventually practiced out of my home. The clients poured in. Emotionally, the "call to service" was extraordinary, like a religious vocation, the kind of vocation I had earlier experienced in the convent. I had no choice but to follow it. I had found a lost piece of myself and felt committed to exploring that part of me. This became my spiritual work. I finally knew what Joseph Campbell meant about the power of myths, when he wrote in *The Hero with a Thousand Faces*, "A hero ventures forth from the world of common day into a region of supernatural wonder."

I was no heroine, but I was beginning to understand "supernatural wonder" and what joy it could bring to me. This bliss began to dissolve the unshed tears I had been unable to release in my grief. The wounds of loss and thwarted love began to heal in wondrous ways.

I put myself out to the public as a psychic and embraced my path knowing I wouldn't return to California nor ever practice law, at least not in the way that I had imagined. I did work in the legal field for many years, but not as the trial lawyer I'd wanted to become. Without the criticism of my mainstream friends and colleagues in California, it seemed like truly divine timing to embark upon this path now. I worked diligently to control the voices, images and imprints that came to me in order to refine and separate the interpretation of the visions into articulate "readings."

The methodology for legal analysis I learned in my first year of law school was called IRAC, an acronym we were taught to use when answering the professor's hypothetical questions regarding the cases we had studied. The acronym stood for Issue, Rule of Law, Application and Conclusion.

(Interestingly, I use this formula now when I read for my clients. There is always a particular Issue that has arisen and the issue is applied to the Rule—which is the client's inner moral compass or the societal rule by which they live. The Rule is then applied to the facts surrounding their issue—Application—and the Conclusion is the outcome or prediction gleaned from the reading. The reading is always about the progression of the client's soul journey).

I don't remember the content of the readings I do after a few hours. However, if a client discusses the reading elsewhere (for instance, on the phone), I can recall some of the information or my guides will simply give me the information again.

In Miami, I gave a disturbing reading in which I predicted that a young woman's brother would be murdered. The girl told me that her brother was heavily into drugs and that her parents were flying into Miami to try to convince him to go into rehab. I told her not to go to his apartment on Thursday, the day she was to pick her mother and father up from the airport and go to her brother's condo for the intervention. I cautioned her that there was violence around him. It was the first time she had come to me, and it was a difficult vision to explain to her.

This was Saturday. The following Thursday, she picked up her parents at the airport. On the way to her brother's apartment (against my advice), a tire went flat and they had to wait on the side of the highway for help. Two hours later than planned, they drove up in front of the condo. The area was blocked off with yellow crime tape. Miami-Dade policemen were still on the scene. Her brother had been murdered in a shootout connected with a drug deal.

When she called to tell me all of this, I asked her if she had believed me when I first informed her about the murder. She said, "Yes, but I knew I had to do this, and I knew somehow I would be protected."

I remember this as an unusual case. She didn't take my advice to stay clear of her brother's place, but instead made the decision to help him, with their parents' assistance, if she could. This made me realize that free will is always an option, and that the reading is always about the person seated in front of me. Her spirit guides protected her even though she failed to heed my advice. She was not caught in the crossfire. She was meant to live.

Other vignettes have happy endings. I read repeatedly for a talented, successful woman in D.C. who couldn't seem to find the kind of man she wanted. I kept telling her that he would be there soon. It took a few years, and her biological clock was ticking away, but he finally came into her life. When he had issues, and she thought he wasn't going to marry her, I told her, "It will change. Just wait, you will marry and birth his son before you know it." Within months, the wedding was planned. Today, she's a happy woman with a newborn son. She confesses now that she couldn't be sure I was the real deal, but her husband is exactly the husband I described.

In other instances, the things I get from the readings seem unlikely. I remember telling a woman that an annoying colleague would leave the office. No one in her workplace believed that would ever happen, but, on cue, the obnoxious person left, right around the date I had predicted she would.

Another time, I helped a friend whose husband had stomach cancer. I told her, upon her request, exactly how many months they had left together, and I predicted his death to the day.

It wasn't until I integrated my own life-changing experiences and processed who I had become that I moved out of the margin into a new state of being. I could recognize my gifts as such and forget the times I had thought I was cursed by knowing what I did not want to know about my husbands, friends and colleagues.

I could finally separate myself from my "bad" mother who killed herself in my swimming pool and remember the "good" mother who was creative, funny, and loved to laugh with her friends and sisters, the good mother I loved and who loved me.

I let go of my critical feelings about my father and my judgment of his weaknesses and remembered him as the emotional man who loved his family more than his own life. My handsome father was a faithful husband to my mother and a steady breadwinner who remained loyal to the same company for forty-two years as he supported us. I felt his unwavering love for our family deep in my heart and loved him deeply in return.

I let go of the alien abduction experience and incorporated the memory into my psyche in order to become who I am today. I still attend Mufon meetings and some International Conventions and read all the literature on UFOs. Spirit moved me recently to the Phoenix area where there have been numerous sightings. That's all there is to say at this time. Who knows what events will occur in future times?

My goal was and is to be the best psychic that I can be and to read in a professional manner, creating a legitimate psychic healing practice in order to serve others by answering my "call to service" unwaveringly.

"We must let go of the life we have planned,
so as to accept the one that is waiting for us."
~Joseph Campbell

Part 3: ALCHEMY

Chapter 15
1990 – St. Vincent, West Indies: Obeah Man

I call myself a Lightrunner™. I use this term rather than the more common word, Lightworker, to describe myself. I was born with wanderlust and was now being guided to trek the world running the Light, meaning to take to others the light of God.

I had always been a traveler, leaving home for the convent in Oregon and then moving to California as a very young woman, traveling extensively with my first husband, and then more simply after getting divorced. Then, with increased income came the opportunity to go where Spirit led as I approached the second half of my life.

I have no angst now about the next step of my journey, no matter where I am called to be or what I am called to do. I simply answer the call. My website chronicles a few of these metaphysical soul journeys.

The paranormal takes many forms. I had an experience in the West Indies that tilted my Pollyanna belief system from impossible to possible. I had much to learn about the world of spirits and my lessons had only begun.

My friend David, whom I met in Jamaica while traveling there with my son, introduced me to the West Indies. I spent time in Jamaica, Barbados, St. Martin and St. Vincent. David was from St. Vincent, and on one trip there, I was invited to a dinner party by a St. Vincent hotelier whose dinner guests included several West Indian couples. What I didn't know until the meal was over was that one of the men there was a West Indian Obeah man and wanted to challenge me in order to pit his skills against mine.

Obeah is a term used in the black magic practiced in Africa and throughout the Caribbean. As a shaman and psychic, an Obeah man generally uses love potions, spells and curses in an attempt to manipulate his clients' wishes so that they become reality. His practice includes healing, divination, and spirit communication. He considers himself a mediator between the world of the living and the spirit world.

The word "shaman" comes from the language of the Siberian Tungus people. The Manchu-tangu origin reached the ethnologic vocabulary through Russian. The word originated from "saman" (xaman), derived from the word "verd-scha" which means "to know." Thus "shaman" means someone who knows, is wise, a sage.

This Obeah man dared me to conjure up an entity for all at the party to see, and I declined. I feel my gifts are not to be used for parlor games. I am dead serious in my endeavor to assist every client on the path he or she has chosen.

I don't recall this gentleman's first name since everyone on the island referred to him as the Obeah man. He was tall and lively, in his late forties. He was native Caribe, but his blood was intermingled with that of generations of Africans that the British had brought to the islands as slaves.

When I refused his request, he jumped up and excused himself from the dinner table for about ten minutes. He returned wearing a long, dark purple robe with gold braid trimming along the front opening. In his hand, he held a thick 8" x 10" book bound in black leather. He opened the book and began to read several detailed incantations. The book was written in cursive and had pen and ink drawings on each page. From where I was seated, I couldn't make out the words but I could see that they were written in English.

I looked at Robbie, my host and friend, and he sent me a look of resignation in return and put a finger to his lips signaling for me to say nothing. After about fifteen minutes of reading, the Obeah man sat and stared silently across the table at me.

Then he said, "You will see that I am more powerful than you, and that I can conjure up images. To prove this to you I will conjure up the devil in this very dining room."

The trade winds gently floated in through the slats in the shuttered windows, and I felt a chill go up the back of my spine and pulsate in the back of my head. I replied, "You need not prove anything to me. I know that you are a respected and loved Obeah man on this island, and I honor you for that achievement. Please! This isn't necessary."

I looked to Robbie for guidance and he lowered his head, which I took as a signal that I was on my own.

I sat like a zombie and watched the next ten or fifteen minutes play out in a most extraordinary way. I didn't think for a minute that this Obeah man could conjure up an image that we could all see, let alone a "devil" image, but on God's honor, that's exactly what the man did.

He rose and walked over to the light switch, turned it off and lit the candles that stood on a nearby sideboard. With only the candlelight and the veranda lights streaming through the wood shutters, the room was in semi-darkness. He again chanted from his large black book, and I began to get first short of breath and then dizzy. I mentally grounded myself with visualizations of angels and mountain air, planting my feet firmly on the floor. I realized that the energy in the room had shifted and the room had grown cold and still.

Next to the sideboard behind Robbie, who sat at the head of the table, a life-size image of an entity—clearly a devil—appeared as if in the flesh.

I gasped. The room filled with the strong stench of the perspiration emitted by the fearful dinner guests. The ceiling fan swirled the noxious odor about the room. The man next to me grabbed my hand and held it tight. I was the only white woman in the room. I felt the glare of the other guests as they focused on my response, although they, like me, seemed terrified.

I wasn't frightened by the devil, likely because, at the time, I didn't subscribe to any belief in evil or in anyone named the "devil." I was in terror at the thought of what else this Obeah man might attempt.

The image lasted almost a full minute. Everyone in the room—all eight dinner guests—saw the representation and identified it as a "devil". He was a cross between man and beast. Red protoplasm surrounded his body. He had black horns, hairy arms, and wore black clothing. He was like no other man I'd ever seen.

I smiled at the Obeah man. I had to give the devil his due.

The Obeah man turned on the lights and the image vanished. The other St. Vincentians appeared thunderstruck, too. He had never performed this feat for them before. Before this night, I'd never met the man—I knew of him only by his reputation—so I wondered if this had been some magic trick, or if I had been the brunt of a sick joke, and they were all in on it.

I conceded. "I could not nor would not desire to do such a thing," I told him. "I work only for the good of the person's soul journey in my practice."

The others were quiet, and I could tell Robbie, as a West Indian, was proud of and impressed by his countryman. This Obeah man had certainly outdone me. I had only practiced readings heretofore. The entire evening, I knew they all thought I was an imposter and that their Obeah man had proved his superiority to me in every way since I refused to take his challenge.

The Obeah man spoke directly to me, "One must work for the all forces to be successful, meaning that one must be open to access the forces of both good and evil. A curse upon another is as powerful as a love potion. I am committed to working with both sides."

I knew this to be true since "thoughts [became] things." If one sent out light and love, the object of that person's thoughts received that energy, so it followed equally that ill will and bad thoughts were also energetically received by the person. Spells must have been transmitted that way. If anything was possible, which I was coming to believe, why was I so resistant to this man's ability to summon the devil?

Later in my hotel room, I pondered the nightmare event and tried to discern whether what I had seen was an illusion, a hologram, or some other type of image projection. Could it possibly have been a flesh and blood "devil" conjured up by the Afro-Caribbean shaman's abilities, as he so claimed?

Emotionally, I felt the image was real, but mentally, I was convinced it was some type of hoax or joke on me. I looked down at the stain from the chocolate dessert sauce I had spilled on the front of my colorful skirt. It was reddish-brown, and I gagged as my stomach churned. It had been upset by the night's events, and the queasiness was further fueled by the spicy goat meat I'd eaten at dinner. Clearly, I had witnessed West Indian "folk magic," believe it or not. Had the Obeah man compelled a shapeshifting spirit to take physical form, and in doing so, had he actualized negative emotional forces into the shape of a demonic or malignant spirit?

Several years later, I came across the idea of a Tulpa, as practiced by Alexandra David-Neel. She was a student of Buddhism who studied in Tibet and wrote several books on mysticism around the 1930s. According to traditional Tibetan doctrines, a Tulpa is an entity created by an act of imagination, rather like the fictional characters created by a novelist, except that the Tulpa is not written down. David-Neel became so interested in the concept that she decided to try to create one. The methodology she used was intense concentration and visualization. David-Neel's Tulpa or psychic phantom existed as a plump, benign little monk, similar to Friar Tuck.

This monk was at first entirely subjective, but gradually, with practice, she was able to visualize the Tulpa as a wraith in the real world. In time, her vision grew in clarity and substance until it seemed a physical reality, much like a self-induced delusion. Before long, the image of Friar Tuck slipped out of her conscious control. The monk would materialize even when she hadn't called him into existence. Moreover, her friendly, round little Friar was slimming down and taking on a distinctly menacing personality apart from her imaginings.

David-Neel's friends, who were unaware of the mental disciplines she was practicing, questioned her about the "stranger" who had turned up in their presence, which indicated that the creature was no longer a creation of her imagination but a definite objective reality.

That was when she decided things had gone too far. She applied different Lama-ist techniques to re-absorb the creature back into her mind. The Tulpa resisted his destruction. The process took several weeks' intense concentration and left David-Neel exhausted. When I read about this I wondered: could the Obeah man's "devil" have been such a Tulpa?

I also happened upon this type of imagery when I was in Thailand. I was staying at the Oriental Hotel in Bangkok and had arranged with a friend in the State Department in Washington D.C. to contact the most famous psychic there. Her name was Yuwaree Wintherpan, and I wanted to do an exchange with her, if she was so inclined.

We met and performed the psychic exchange, which itself was an extraordinary occurrence. We used a translator (a male friend of hers) since I did not speak Thai, nor she English. We each did a one-hour reading for the other. The first thing I "saw" around her were bolts of red silk being cut for a special gown for her upcoming wedding. I saw her wearing the dress at the wedding altar. The translator told me later that Yuwaree was planning a second wedding with an East Indian man, and that she had been buying bolts of red silk the day before at the fabric store for one of the gowns she would wear at the wedding. I don't remember what else I told her, but she seemed happy about the content of my reading. I remember the red silk since the translator and I discussed the reading. He also told me that she was immediately impressed by my accuracy.

Yuwaree saw my deceased father in his physical form and described him during her reading. She saw him standing tall and erect but with his left arm flailing at his side. Daddy had suffered a stroke and had lost control of his left arm as a result. She saw his dark hair flecked with gray and the distinct Fu Manchu mustache that my sisters carefully trimmed and nurtured. She described him in such detail that I knew my father was in the room with me. During World War II, Dad had been stationed in the Marianna Islands where the Americans had fought against the Japanese. He wouldn't have wanted me to be traveling around the world on my own, especially in Asia, as I so often did, so he must have been trying to protect me.

However, what I found most interesting were the secondhand stories I heard from the hotel staff and my friends in the State Department. They relayed that anyone receiving a reading from Yuwaree in her house waited first on a bench inside the foyer downstairs for a while as she read upstairs. A monk waited with them on the bench, but this monk never spoke with the clients.

The elderly monk with shaved head and saffron robes would sit beside the client until Yuwaree came to the stairwell and called the client to come upstairs to join her for the reading. One particular trusted friend in the State Department, whom I shall call Barbara, had lived in Thailand and had been to the psychic for a reading. She had seen the monk on the bench. I trusted her account of this vision.

I asked the Thai reader about the monk, and she said to me via a translator, "Oh, that's my spirit guide. He protects me because I'm alone in my home when I do readings. He comes and goes." I, too, have a gatekeeper who assists me in my readings—St. Anne of Cleves—but she never sits in my long vestibule. Was this "spirit guide" another instance of a Tulpa?

The Thai reader and her male translator friend took me under their wings during the rest of my trip, escorting me to dinner and arranging sightseeing trips. They also drove me to the airport on my last day. The translator gave me his gold amulet to wear around my neck. I felt well protected.

Yuwaree commented to me as she hugged me goodbye, "Your father asked me to protect you, and so we have." I was treated like royalty because I had been recognized as a friend of the most famous reader in Thailand. Word had spread throughout the hotel because she, along with her entourage, had met me in the lobby several times. Clasped hands and elaborate bows greeted me during the rest of my stay everywhere I went: in the lobby, near the elevator, in the restaurants and bars. The massage therapists and the aestheticians at the spa argued over who would wait on me. My father, in his wisdom from the other side, had no doubt found me just the right protector.

I was learning that there is much more to this world than meets the eye, but also that sometimes, there are things that *do* meet the eye, when summoned.

Chapter 16
1991 – Alexandria, VA: Apparitions

In 1991, I relocated from Miami to Old Town Alexandria, Virginia, settling into a historical home by the river. Remember my friend and psychic Eloise, from San Francisco? What she predicted came true. Alexandria was the "town with cobblestone streets" that "started with an A." A woman named Ann drove a horse and buggy along the river for tourists. She parked her buggy next door when it wasn't in use, and I was friendly with her. This too, had been one of Eloise's predictions. I was startled when I realized this. My plan had originally been to live in D.C., but I looked at the two-hundred-year-old house and fell in love with it and Alexandria.

The house was saturated with the energy of an old woman, a deceased benevolent spirit that I loved. However the walls of the house contained black mold spores that caused me agonizing respiratory problems and bouts of pneumonia. Although I was aware that the house was overly damp, I believed I'd be alright and the spirit would keep me healthy. I wasn't and she didn't, so I moved.

This new residence was a condominium, still in Old Town Alexandria, situated diagonally across from a Catholic elementary school. From my private patio, I could see a large white statute of the Blessed Virgin on the front lawn of the school. From the French doors in my living room I could also see a lovely cupola on the rooftop. Viewed through the greenery of a majestic tree planted in the middle of my ground floor patio, this scene was a pleasing one. It made me remember the devotion I once felt for the Blessed Virgin of my youth.

I located the rosary that I had purchased in Bethlehem during a Catholic moment, and left it on my nightstand. I recalled that the nuns used to tell us wonderful stories about "the children of Fatima." In Portugal, 1917, a luminous apparition of the Virgin Mary appeared to three peasant children and delivered a prophecy to be revealed in 1960. However, when the time came, the College of Cardinals at the Vatican convened, and the message was not publicized. Later, it was determined that Pope Paul VI had decided not to reveal Fatima's message. I could only surmise his reasons.

My rage had been diluted and my anger at God diminished as I sought community and counsel at the Institute for Spiritual Development (ISD) in Washington, D.C. as well as at the Institute for the Advancement of Service (IAS) in Alexandria.

I set up an appointment for my first client in my new house. After introductions, I began the reading. When I looked into her aura, I thought I was losing it. I saw clearly an image of the Blessed Virgin hovering above her in a blue and white gown. Often, I see Spirit guides or dead relatives during readings, but this image of the Blessed Virgin seemed to be my own projection triggered by the schoolyard statue across the street. I continued with the reading, trying to ignore it. The image began to vibrate, the signal I always got from my gatekeeper that I needed to inform my client about it. Now I had to tell her what I saw.

"Do you have any connection to the Catholic Blessed Virgin? I see an image of her above you. She is smiling and happy that you have come to me," I said.

The woman opened her purse and pulled out her rosary before she replied, "I have a special devotion to Mary; I say the rosary every day." She opened the collar of her blouse to reveal a silver chain from which dangled a Catholic medallion with the Blessed Mother engraved on it. The pose was the same as the one I saw above her.

I took this incident as a means of keeping me in line. The lesson for me was clear: whenever I think I'm seeing things that can't be so during a reading (or that it's my own projection because it's so bizarre) and I'm not sure if I should repeat what comes to me, I, Susan, hesitate a moment, and my gatekeeper nudges me, "Repeat it; it comes from Spirit, not you." My ego gets taken down a peg to remind me that it is not I who speaks—I am a medium and the message is spoken through me. I am only an instrument for relaying it.

A few years later, an acquaintance of mine called to say that she and a few friends were going to Emmitsburg, Maryland, to see a young woman who had been receiving messages from the Blessed Virgin. The Catholic Church was treating the apparitions as authentic. Did I want to go? I was secretly amused by this, since I'd never told anyone about my own visitations from the Blessed Virgin as a child. The friend simply thought I might be interested as a psychic.

As we seated ourselves in St Joseph's Church in Emmitsburg on Thursday evening, I could see the young woman, Gianna Talone Sullivan, kneeling at the altar waiting for Mass to end and the apparitions to commence. I was eager to hear her message from the Blessed Virgin. The Church was filled to overflowing. Between 600 and 1,000 people had been in attendance each week, and tonight was no exception.

Gianna listened intently and at times communicated with the Virgin in a soft voice that we could only faintly hear. When she finished, the parish priest took the microphone and relayed the message sentence by sentence. I was taken aback to see this. It seemed wrong that she had to tell the priest her message from Mary so that he could convey it to the audience. She was an educated pharmacist, so I couldn't fathom why she wasn't allowed to speak for herself; it was upsetting to me.

I was immediately suspicious—not of her—but of the Catholic Church who obviously wanted to filter or monitor what she said. I resented the male hierarchy of the church. Either this man, or his superiors, had decided that only a priest could relay the message from the Blessed Virgin when in fact Our Lady had chosen Gianna for the purpose.

Gianna appeared to be channeling the information, and since I had seen several channelers in Miami—including Ramtha, Lazarus, Mataare, and my own sister, Gloria—I was most interested in the phenomena. She acted like other trance channelers I'd seen who received information telepathically and didn't contort their bodies or change expression no matter how deep the trance. It took concentration to remain still and quiet, to stay focused on what was going on in her head. It was the same as doing a reading. During a reading, I heard only the person in front of me, saw images in my head and listened to the voices speaking to me. In a state of "knowingness," the information came to me.

Gianna appeared to be authentic, and the messages I heard that night were benevolent, always beginning with: "My dear little children, praise be to Jesus."

The parish had added on a large hall to the church to accommodate the hundreds of visitors, like us, who came from afar. We spent time in this center and met others who were enamored with the visions of Gianna. Nearly everyone we met concurred that they believed she was truly speaking with the Blessed Virgin.

The service was also interesting because it was conducted by the Catholic Church, which at that time was petitioning The Vatican for the authorization to continue these special services. Everything underwent investigation, from Gianna's years lived in Arizona, where the visions began, to the years since her move to Emmitsburg in 1993, when she and her husband joined St. Joseph's Parish. The collected messages spanned the period from November 3, 1993 to March 30, 1995. They were put into booklet form by

Frank Tighe from Taneytown, Maryland. I read them carefully.

Unfortunately, on September 8, 2000, the Archdiocese of Baltimore issued a statement with the approval of Cardinal William H. Keeler, indicating that it "[found] no basis" for the alleged apparitions or messages of the Blessed Virgin Mary that Gianna Talone Sullivan claimed to receive during prayer services at St. Joseph's in Emmitsburg. The prayer services were shut down, despite the hundreds of faithfuls who had traveled long distances to hear the messages. Gianna and her physician husband, Michael, obeyed the Bishop and stopped disseminating the information.

As I pondered the nature of our apparitions—mine and Gianna's—I looked inward at my past and the Catholic family from which I had gleaned my values. We had all attended Catholic schools and were a religious family. I was close to each of my six siblings, or so I thought, but one of them, Margaret (Margie), who is as sweet as an angel, shifted her beliefs to what I call "the Christian Right." She doesn't go to doctors or celebrate holidays or birthdays, yet I continue to think of her every March 20th, the day she was born.

She now calls and checks on me periodically. She intimates that I'm doing what she considers to be the "devil's" work, yet she reads my website and desires to discuss the content. I want to call her, but each time I do so, she's on a mission to convert me. I think she wishes for all her siblings to be with her in Paradise and believes we're all lost due to our metaphysical beliefs and Catholic baptisms.

I think of her often and pray that we can reconnect, if not on this earth, then in the next life. I'm sure her impression of my beliefs is that they are as extreme as I think hers are. We say the same things and interpret them differently. I receive information from higher entities; she speaks in tongues. Are we not both channeling someone or something? I believe that we are both of the Light. She's a wonderful, loving, joyous person and a pleasure to be around when she's not on a mission to make me convert to her beliefs.

Even though I still "see Mary," I just can't go back.

Chapter 17
2002 – Cap Haitian, Haiti: Voodoo in Paradise

Spirit had still more lessons to teach me. A few years later, I had the opportunity to take a trip to Haiti with two new friends who'd known each other in Italy. I first met them in Washington D.C. after I moved to the suburb of Alexandria.

On a whim, my Scottish friend, Kiki, had called me. "Didn't you tell me once that you longed to go to Haiti? Well I'm going. Do you want to join Donatella and me?"

"Yes!" I shrieked. "When?"

Sun, friends, the beach, swimming, and lounging in hammocks with no phone, no TV, no e-mail and no work beckoned; I couldn't resist the invitation to stay at the Hotel Cormier Plage strategically situated on a cove facing the sea.

The ticket agent at Lynx Aviation in Florida took my passage for Haiti and called out my name, prompting me to stand on the luggage rack to be weighed as a passenger for the aircraft.

"145 pounds, female," the man called to his female co-worker at the other end of the counter. She logged the information in a large black ledger for the captain of the aircraft. Sheesh! Weights and balances I understood, but to be so indiscreet! Next to my friend Donatella (whose weigh-in preceded mine at ninety-nine pounds) my weight made me feel like an elephant, and I lumbered down the jet-way.

"Oh darling, don't worry! It took a month of dieting to get my weight under 100 pounds," she consoled in her alluring Italian accent. I glanced at Kiki, who was trying to hide a smirk. Kiki was fluent in Italian since she had lived in Rome for many years.

*You **would** smirk. You're a well-shaped, "skinny" woman, too,* I groused inwardly.

Soon we were aboard the small aircraft and high above the clouds on our way to Haiti. The sky was a brilliant blue, and with the promise of a week in the sun ahead of us, we were jubilant.

Donatella was fidgety, "I can't wait to see Jean-Bernard. I love him! I miss him so!" she lamented for the fifth time.

"He is such a sweetheart," I agreed.

As the captain guided the Fairchild Metro-liner III into its descent, I could see the beach and a narrow strip of concrete that looked like a gleaming bike trail running between the masses of green foliage that surrounded the landing strip for Cap Haitian, Haiti's northernmost city. There was not one body lying on the amazing white sand beach. I couldn't wait to hear the sound of the waves, smell the salt air, and enjoy the solitude. I heard the landing gear disengage, and then we touched down on the runway. All nineteen of us passengers cheered.

Overpowering body odor carried by the trade winds along with a hint of frangipani swirled in my nostrils as we deplaned and ran for the makeshift hangar. We were anxious to clear customs and find the ladies' room since we had been without a "facility" on our three-hour flight from Florida. "What? No bottled water or food? No bathroom? What would we do if we had a bathroom emergency?" we'd complained.

Jean-Claude, his wife Kathy, and her son, Jean-Bernard, were each uniquely different and amazing hosts. French by origin, they had been in Haiti for almost twenty years and hadn't lost that unique French flair that encompassed everything from fabulous cooking to a colorful, tropical sense of style. Jean-Bernard met us at the airport and took us to the hotel.

He drove the Land Rover from town over roads with potholes that rivaled those in our nation's Capital. Tin corrugated shacks lined the roadside shoulder-to-shoulder with once-beautiful buildings, their architecture crumbling with decay as the colonial past was also laid to waste. The aggression and violence associated with the poverty of Haiti that I had read about was nowhere to be seen. Instead, everywhere I looked, I saw serenity, peacefulness and acceptance on its smiling faces.

Wide-eyed, black-skinned children waved at us and called out to Jean-Bernard as he drove. Donatella was thrilled to see Jean-Bernard and sat next to him in the front seat, gushing sweet lovers' talk the entire way.

We headed south toward the cove. As we wove our way inland from the sea and climbed the mountains, we passed villages where women knelt in dresses or skirts to scrub their family's clothes in streams that traveled down the mountainsides and out to sea. Bright yellow, blue and orange-colored cotton dresses and boy's shorts and shirts in hues of green and blue, all sizes, were spread to dry on banana leaves, covering the dark green foliage like spots on a leopard.

Brown-eyed children carried stained Clorox bottles and plastic milk jugs to the springs to retrieve their family's water supply for the day. Some of the children, still toddlers, stumbled, spilling the water along the way.

When we reached it, bougainvillea vines and vegetation in various shades of green interspersed with bursts of yellow and red, lined the hotel property. My room faced the sea just a few feet from the sand. The balcony held two large wicker chairs and a rectangular wooden coffee table barely large enough to hold a book, my evening tea (or wine), and bare feet.

After a delightful lunch of fresh red snapper grilled to perfection and served under a bamboo-thatch, in an open-air dining room facing the ocean, I knew I'd come to the right place. Lobster, sea urchins, Buerre Blanc sauce, and warm desserts prepared only the way the French can, were the order of the day. The conversation drifted in French, Italian, and then English for my benefit.

Daily, I sat in the comfortable wicker chair a few feet inland from the sea on my balcony or snuggled in the hammock that hung from a spindly tree in the sand near the ocean's edge listening to the waves that lapped the shore. I swam with the tides, careening in the surf. I needed no air conditioning; ceiling fans dissuaded the mosquitoes. Small green geckos climbed the wall by day and winged insects fluttered about at night. I felt secure in the still darkness and let the trade winds coo me to sleep.

Nevertheless, I was soon challenged to leave my hammock. Jean-Bernard, at my coaxing, had been working with the locals from Cap to see if we could do what I had heretofore only dreamed of. I had always longed to attend an authentic voodoo ceremony performed by a real priest with real followers, no tourists allowed, with me and my companions as the only invited guests. After a few days of negotiations, we agreed to pay for the rum to be consumed by the voodoo priest, provide four chickens with which to feed the crowd, and cover a few other incidentals to be paid to the right folks. We were all set to attend the ceremony.

The day arrived and we were apprehensive. Donatella said, "Maybe we should forget the whole idea, what if something happens, and we can't control it? I'm getting nervous." I was determined to attend regardless.

Only a few stars glittered in the inky black sky. We—Jean-Bernard, Donatella, Kiki and me, plus our local guide—a former member of the *Tonton Macoute* from Duvalier's regime whose name escaped me in the translated introduction—traveled for miles past Cap, bumping along rutted dirt roads in the Land Rover. Jean-Bernard trusted the guide who had arranged the logistics for the night we would spend in

attendance at the most fascinating of all Haitian traditions—
the Voodoo Ceremony.

We three women were disoriented after we left Cap
and couldn't tell in what direction we headed. We could hear
distant drumming, and, as it grew steadily louder, the guide
asked Jean-Bernard to stop the car. The two of them left us
sitting in the Land Rover. Jean-Bernard cautioned us only
once before they left. "Stay in the car. No matter what, do *not*
get out of the car. Understood? No matter what happens.
Someone will come for you, but stay in the car if I don't
come back."

We were glued to our seats. Kiki took my hand and
began to pray in a feeble voice, "Hail Mary full of grace…"

Donatella and I joined in, "The Lord is with Thee…"

"What's going on in there? Are you chanting? Get out
of the car." Jean-Bernard pounded on the window to get us
to open the door we had locked.

"We're three scared former Catholic school girls
reciting our prayers," Donatella muttered.

"For God's sake, get a grip! You all agreed to do
this." Jean-Bernard could see that we were holding hands and
truly frightened. We were surrounded by blackness, no lights
in the distance, no houses, or at least none with electricity. He
helped us from the Rover to the dirt road and told us to hold
hands until we reached the ceremony site.

"Remember what we talked about this afternoon.
Don't try to insinuate yourselves into the ceremony. Even if
you're asked to dance, stay in your places. Sit tight in the
plastic chairs I insisted they bring for us. We are the only
guests and the only non-Haitians here. We are privileged. Be
respectful, but do not, and I mean *do not*, start swaying to the
music and do not get up to follow in the dancing. I mean it.
Stay seated at all times."

We didn't say a word as we followed him across the
road. We ran into clucking chickens, a small goat, and two

children holding hands before we came to a large meadow overgrown with spiky grass. We walked further into the clearing, and I could see a fire burning at its center. A majestic tree that looked like an oak bordered the clearing. Near it was a lean-to shack open along the front with a dirt porch. The drummers were stationed along the length of the porch, and their beat was slow and steady. Haitian villagers stood or squatted around the periphery of the area. Directly across from the porch on the other side of the fire sat four plastic chairs that faced the ceremonial site. The *Tonton Macoute* guide motioned for us to sit in them.

I counted everyone around the campfire as a means of controlling my anxiety. Somewhere around thirty-five people milled about the circumference. There were no children in the dirt courtyard.

A man I thought to be in his late fifties came forward and began to draw on the dirt floor that backed up to the low-rise structure. With exact precision, he etched the *"veve,"* a ceremonial drawing that would invoke the Loa Guine (The Spirit). He held what I thought was a candle. I wondered if our money had purchased it. Later, I asked Jean-Bernard about it and he said, "No, what you saw was an ox tendon, twisted and dried, then lit as a candle."

The man spoke softly in Haitian Creole, and it was evident that he was the priest or *houngan,* the one who would be the gatekeeper to the Spirit world. The *houngan* incorporated traditional elements of the design I had seen in books as he drew, but his own creativity was also evident. He walked the perimeter of the porch or *peristyle* adjacent to the dirt altar chamber, the *hounfor.* He took his time and drew with a branch using a powder-like substance—perhaps cornmeal or wood ash—to illuminate the crevices in the dirt. He prayed the Catholic "Our Father," in Creole or a *patois* of sorts with all the incantations of a Latin mass.

The fire burned higher and brighter as he stood watch over each symbol he created, preparing the ceremonial space.

Two inner circles were drawn and star points added to them, making them look like pentacles. Then he added another set of symbols along the edge of the area in front of the drummers. A *poto mitan*, or large pole, that represented the spiritual center and supported the spirit house was thrust into the ground to the left of the two *veve* markings.

The chickens squawked as though they knew their fate when the *houngan* stooped to pick up a skinny one that pecked at his foot. With one quick twist, he broke its neck. The chicken's head plopped to one side and blood splattered the priest and us, his shocked audience. He put his mouth to the chicken's neck and made sucking sounds as its blood smeared his face. He wiped the blood away before taking a drink of rum.

"We have the best seats in the house, and now I know why," Kiki whispered when she felt the warm blood spatter.

The priest downed another swallow of rum, and the drummers' syncopated rhythm sped up, stimulating the quiet group of Haitians to movement. Several women stepped around the symbols within the *veve* and began to swish their skirts back and forth, gracefully swaying to the beat of the music. A few men joined in, gyrating their hips and thrusting their abdomens forward provocatively. The priest kept drinking his rum as the tempo increased again. Unseen entities floated around the campfire just waiting to possess a wanting soul.

After an hour or so of continuous movement, the dancers began to jerk erratically as though they were puppets on strings. Sweat poured down the faces of the men, and the women in their handmade dresses and colorful skirts lost their gracefulness as they, too, wilted with perspiration. It was apparent that the Loa had begun to "ride" their heads. (The person is regarded as a horse in French, *cheval;* the Loa rides the "horse" or person.) The *houngan* chanted and prayed in

French Creole, mostly unintelligible to me. Then another chicken lost its life.

Donatella gasped. "How many chickens are going to die?"

The shock in the front row was the same as if we had not already seen this happen once before, and we sat spellbound in the humid night air, splattered with blood, watching the flames, the dancing, and the Loa's possession of his followers.

I leaned toward Kiki and teased, "Don't you want to dance?" Jean-Bernard heard me and gave me a stern look. Donatella began to sway with the music, and Jean-Bernard poked her so she would be still. Kiki and I dared not look at one another for fear of giggling hysterically. That might cause us to be dragged into the dance where we would be possessed, or worse, sacrificed to the fire.

Feathers floated around us. The chickens must have been plucked by the invisible hands that also cut them up and readied them for the coals one by one. Two more chicken necks cracked, making a total of four dead fowl. The disembodied spirits, according to custom, grew tired and worn down by the hard task of running the universe. They relied then on humans to "feed" them via the periodic rituals and animals sacrifices. Goats and pigs were also sacrificed, but in this small village that night, we saw only chickens being used.

One female dancer who seemed to be enjoying the music as she swayed to the rhythm and clapped her hands fell to the ground sputtering, and when she arose, her attitude was completely different. She was no longer an innocent. She kept swiveling her hips in an overtly sexual manner until a handsome man came from the shadows to match her movements.

As I watched, a large woman with flowing hair came to me. In a gruff man's voice she said, "Come dance with me," or at least, that's what I guessed she said. Pantomiming, she tugged at my hands.

"No, no." I shook my head and held fast to the seat of my chair so she couldn't pull me off it.

I was trying to heed Jean-Bernard's instructions to stay seated and was a bit anxious. I knew that if a male spirit mounts a female, she would be called a "he" during the ceremony. He/she kept chiding me to dance.

Perhaps the male entity that had invaded the Haitian woman manipulated my feelings by transferring his dark, negative energy into my aura. Or, I was already so caught up in the sociological experiment we were engaged in by attending the ceremony that my aura was weakened. Abrupt behavioral change is a common symptom of an entity trying to psychically attack the person. At first, I had no intention of getting caught up in the drama, and then I desperately desired to join the merrymakers.

Whatever the reason, I suddenly wanted to stand up and dance with her, but Jean-Bernard spoke sternly in French, and he/she let me go. I didn't understand why Jean-Bernard was so adamant that we abstain. Later, I realized that it was because he was afraid that our own spirits would be possessed.

While this was going on, Donatella joined the circle of women as if in a trance. Kiki and I sat frozen in place as we watched Donatella move with the group, first with a woman, and then with a man who took her small frame in his arms and pulled her to him. Jean-Bernard yelled, "Get over here and sit down, right now!"

She ignored him. He stood up and pulled her from the circle. Donatella plunked into her chair and muttered, "Let me dance! I was having fun." Jean-Bernard held her arm so she couldn't move from her chair, and we all sat for a long time without batting an eyelash.

I felt woozy as the villagers continued their frenzy that was no longer a dance. It was now a sea of bodies being "ridden" by the Loa. The smoke from the open fire, along with the pungent body odor and strong smell of rum made it difficult to discern who was with whom as they moved in a circle around the *veve*.

The *houngan* called on individuals, and in return, they called out requests of the Spirits. One asked Loa Guine, "Please cure my baby," and another called to the Loa, "Heal my husband! He is dying, and what will become of me?" Some were clear petitions, but others were garbled to me because of the mix of French Creole they used.

The night wore on and the music continued, the villagers danced and the drummers continued to up the tempo. Long before midnight, the energy turned explicitly sexual and although the voyeur in me wanted to stay, I felt emotionally drained. The others, too, grew weary and we exchanged nods of quiet agreement that it was time to leave. The guide took us women to our vehicle and locked us inside while he stood guard beside the road.

Jean-Bernard lingered awhile longer behind us in order to thank our host and convey our appreciation for the invitation to the ceremony. When he joined us, we drove away with drums pounding in our ears and visions of the Loa in our heads.

I was not the only one who understood the unseen. Because of what I had witnessed that night, I discovered there were entire cultures that embraced the unknown freely and without shame.

Part 4: CHRYSALIS

Chapter 18
2005 – Alexandria, VA: Life Lessons

The terrorist attack on the World Trade Center in New York City on September 11, 2001, shook America to its core. Millions saw the live broadcast as two jet liners crashed into the twin towers. We watched as the people jumped to their deaths below, and scattered bits and pieces of the destruction swirled in a kaleidoscope of emotional pain that seared our collective consciousness. I could see the roiling clouds of black smoke from the Pentagon when it was hit in the second assault, as I stood in the street outside my home in Alexandria. Passengers attempted to thwart-the third terrorist attack aboard an aircraft that crashed in Shanksville, Pennsylvania, killing everyone. The events of 9/11 changed Americans forever, myself included.

My thriving psychic practice kept me tuned into Spirit. I was deep into Jungian shadow work as an analysand: my spiritual work; my readings and workshops; and my seeker's heart sang to be globetrotting full tilt when fate intervened in the form of tumors in my breast.

Before this, I had not felt any lumps in my breasts nor was there a history of breast cancer in my family. I only suffered the yearly mammograms because I had insurance and thought they were something I should have.

I knew immediately from the way the radiologist spoke to me that my body had changed from healthy to diseased, that I had cancer. He said, "There are a couple of spots we need to watch on your right side, but usually, these spots aren't the kind that are cancerous. However, there's another spot there that your doctor might want to test further, or he might schedule a biopsy."

I asked, "Who's the best breast cancer surgeon around here?"

He gave me a name without hesitation. I wrote it down and put the slip of paper in my purse.

No one from my doctor's office called me. Not that day or the next, or the next. On the third day after my mammogram appointment, I called the radiologist back. He told me he'd sent the report to my gynecologist the day I'd been in to see him and that I should have been contacted by now.

I called the gynecologist's office and left a message. There was no return call—ever.

I contacted the surgeon that the radiologist recommended and said I needed an appointment. I fibbed and told his receptionist that I had been referred by my gynecologist. Then I called the radiologist and asked him to send the records to the surgeon. In the interim, I researched the surgeon on my office computer. He was head of the cancer department at a nearby hospital and had sterling credentials.

That afternoon, the receptionist from the surgeon's office left this message on my office voice mail: "Please call our office as soon as you receive this message. You need to see the surgeon immediately. Your mammogram shows that you have cancer in several locations on your right breast." I later found out that she had assumed that my gynecologist had spoken with me already or she wouldn't have left such a message.

My gynecologist, Amy, was a vibrant young doctor in whom I had complete faith.

That was my first mistake.

I'm still waiting for her to call me back to inform me that I have cancer. It's been four and a half years since I had a mastectomy on my right side. I never got around to confronting the remiss doctor. Although one of my

167

colleagues in the office said to me later, that I had told her as I was going out the door for my appointment that I was upset because I thought I had cancer. I do not remember the conversation nor can imagine that I would tell someone that kind of premonition. Yet she still insists that I said that to her. I was likely thinking that and getting it psychically but did not know that I said it aloud.

My life was turned upside down as I tried to cope with life-threatening cancer and work, while my family was still on the west coast and I was far away from their support in the mid-Atlantic area of the country.

I obtained a new gynecologist who aided me in my recovery. The surgeon sent me to get my records from Dr. Amy's office; the mammogram results were listed on the first page in the file. Clearly, I had fallen through the cracks. The radiology report had no notes attached to it—no reminders to call the patient or take any other action.

I was fortunate the cancer was found early. There were two different types of it in three locations that left no doubt that the breast had to be removed. I was counseled to have a mastectomy, unless I wanted to be left with a breast that resembled Swiss cheese. The mastectomy and subsequent eighteen months of reconstruction are not something I ever want to repeat.

I didn't have radiation or chemo, but I was instead advised to take the drug, Femara, for five years. I took Femara for two-and-a-half years, until I could tolerate it no longer. I had already tried Arimedex but couldn't get the side effect of constant vomiting under control. My cancer was hormone receptive, which meant that taking a hormone suppressing drug was the common protocol. I felt lucky; lucky enough to tempt fate and discontinue the Femara.

That was my second mistake.

I had planned to visit my brother Robb in Brookings, Oregon, where he had retired. His health had been failing ever since he'd undergone bypass surgery and had subsequent problems. My son said that he'd go with me, but my health issues prevented it. Then it was too late, Robb was dying.

Because I was so many miles away, I said my goodbyes to him via Skype, something not even thought of when I was born. Through this then-new computer technology, my brother, Ed, facilitated the conference call. Those of us who weren't able to be there with him in person were able to speak with Robb and see him in his hospital room individually while the other siblings chatted, and he was able to see and speak to us privately.

My sister Ananfaye commented, "It was a profound experience."

My Robbie, the older brother I adored; the one I tagged after and tried to be like when I was little; the one I thought was my mother's favorite because she let him stay up later at night than she did me; the one I thought had all the adventures because he was a boy; the one who loved cars and tinkered with them every spare moment; the one who delighted in teasing us, his sisters—was dead. The complications of his bypass surgery had taken him from us.

My sisters and I used to wrestle Robb to the floor and wave our long hair in his face (which he hated) to get even with him when he taunted us. Robb taught me to ride my bike and spoke out against my boyfriends because he didn't think any of them were good enough for me. He was a Navy man, a sailor, an artist, a hunter, a fisherman, a restaurateur, a shop owner, a businessman, a teasing uncle to my children and a loving father to his own three children. He adored his wife, my sister-in-law, Linda, for over fifty years.

As adults, we had lived on the same street in California for awhile. He used to walk over on weekends to visit. On one occasion, we talked about what we really wanted in a career and he said, "Susan, if I had to do it all over again, I would have gone to college and become an Oceanographer instead of joining the Navy." Surprised, I confessed that I

169

wished I had pursued that early dream myself. The marine world fascinated him his entire life, as it still does me. He is buried on a lovely, grassy knoll overlooking the Pacific Ocean so that he may always be near his beloved sea.

I thought, *Farewell, dear brother. You have crossed the threshold into another dimension, into God's Light. Mother and Daddy, I am confident you are there waiting for him. Your spirit, big brother, will always be with me.*

I believed Mom would be there to meet him, too, because, when she committed suicide, Robb told me, "She changed her mind, I know she did, but it was too late." He believed that the ropes with which she had tied herself to the chair prevented her from surfacing and grasping onto life. He said he had to believe that she must have wanted to live at the last second.

The loss of my brother made me sad that we had lived so far from one another and had not stayed in touch often enough. When I confronted cancer, I changed. I lived, worked, and traveled more. I wanted to see and do everything possible to fulfill my "bucket list" before something happened and I got sick, the cancer came back, or life became too fragile. Robb's death was also a reminder to me to live life to its fullest.

Chapter 19
January, 2010 – Phoenix, AZ: Cancer: Twice

Thinking of my future as a single woman, I decided to look for property that I could purchase either for resale or to live in when I retired. I didn't want to live anywhere there was snow. I loved to ski for pleasure, but the hassle of a Mid Atlantic winter had become too much for me. I'd originally considered buying in The Quarter in New Orleans, since I loved the city and believed it would be an ideal place in which to live and host my clientele as a psychic.

However, Spirit led me to choose the Phoenix area. I say "led" because the best thing about being psychic is that I always know what to do in a given moment—not that my decisions are always perfect, but I do feel my spiritual guides and my dead parents are looking out for my well-being and are giving me the best signals they can.

So, following my ethereal direction, I purchased a home in the Phoenix suburbs, rented it out for the first two winters, and forgot about New Orleans. I was a westerner who wanted to be near San Francisco and Phoenix since my children were now living there. Escrow closed in May, 2004, prior to the housing boom and subsequent bust and prior to Katrina, the violent hurricane that devastated New Orleans in August, 2005.

I thanked my spiritual guides for their protection. I wouldn't have bought any house had I known I would get cancer and have a mastectomy in 2005 or that Katrina would eliminate one of my choices.

Unable to meet the five-year mark, I was diagnosed with a new cancer on my left breast, my second bout. Fear overwhelmed me, like ocean waves crashing relentlessly upon the shore. No matter what I did, the waves came, and each time, I relived the feelings of helplessness.

After four-and-a-half years, the second time around was definitely different. I was positive and humbled to be alive the first time. This time, I just wanted it to be over and despair engulfed me at the oddest moments. I was filled with anxiety, the opposite of my usual composure, and I couldn't help but ask the silent, terrified questions, "What if they can't stop it this time? What if I die this time?"

I couldn't cry. My tears had dried up a long time ago. I swallowed them, pushed them down deep inside me, and there was no way to release them now. Instead, I sank into the "poor, poor, pitiful me" syndrome. No matter how much I strove to be positive and attempted to think healthy, happy thoughts, I was despondent.

First, I had a core biopsy and then a lumpectomy—or a partial mastectomy, as the doctor called it. Even when these procedures were finished, the horror remained a constant companion.

The only good thing was that my treatment this time was radically easier than the mastectomy surgery I underwent the first time. I'd changed, or else the procedure of an "ice cream scoop" was different—the pain was not so agonizing, and the recovery was speedier. Three weeks out, there was still some mild discomfort in the form of an odd pain in both my lymph nodes and breast, but it didn't last. I was told the pain was likely due to the regeneration of my nerve endings. The thought of sprouting new nerves comforted me.

My radiation decision was unique, so I kept a diary of the five days I spent in radiation therapy that I choose to share with my readers because not everyone is given the same facts or options regarding their treatment, and others going through this will be able to relate.

My doctor recommended radiation after he received the pathology of my tumor. My cancer was early stage, an infiltrating ductal carcinoma with no lymph node involvement, and it was also hormone receptive. I considered myself lucky. These factors, coupled with other criteria such as its size—not exceeding 3.0 cm—and type—no distant metastases—made me a candidate for brachytherapy, so he sent me to a radiation oncologist to discuss my options.

Dr. T., the radiation oncologist, was incredible. We discussed radiation. She was quite knowledgeable and spent time showing me the various applicators that might be temporarily implanted into my breast for the delivery of the treatment. My device was to be a Savi™ breast brachytherapy device. She explained that the doctors liked to do the implant within about four weeks of the partial mastectomy while the cavity was still open and scar tissue hadn't formed in an effort to close it.

Dr. T. answered all my questions about the procedure and told me what my diet would be during radiation. She asked me not to take the supplements that I usually took, since any form of antioxidant would interfere with the process. (I had planned to take heavy doses of vitamin C during treatment, but, nixed that upon her advice.) She sent me home with a lot to ponder. I eagerly researched all I could find on the internal radiation delivery and its various systems. I also researched the Savi™ applicator on the Internet, but the information I found was limited.

My first question was: did I want to spend seven weeks (or 33 treatments) of my life commuting two hours a day—prolonging the anxiety and discomfort—or condense it to five days in one week, with high doses of internal targeted radiation focused on the cancer? Both options would leave me fatigued and depressed. My next question was: did I want to put my life on hold, skipping spring in Arizona, staying out of the swimming pool, missing my water aerobics, unable to enjoy my morning walks, too tired to move?

Which type of radiation I should submit my breast and my body to? Both would cause disruption to my life. After considering my options—either external beam radiation for seven weeks or internal targeted radiation for five days—I decided that the five-day treatment was the safest plan for me. I fit the criteria, my surgeon was skilled at inserting the device, and I had a radiation oncologist who was familiar with the procedure.

In contrast to the targeted brachytherapy radiation, beam radiation just didn't seem to me to be as well controlled. Since my left side was involved, I was worried about the possible damage to my heart that could occur in addition to the damage to my lungs and ribs (which would occur in either case). From what I'd read, internal radiation was equally as effective and would cause minimal damage to my other organs.

My decision also centered on another issue. I'd had two other biopsies on the same breast, which were deemed benign. Was it really better to dose the whole breast with external beam radiation since the beam and dosage could wipe out these calcifications that might somehow turn into cancerous tumors? There was this positive aspect to consider concerning the beam radiation.

I made my decision after consulting with my team; the oncologist, the surgeon and the oncology radiologist. I debated the issue for two days, concluding that the cancer could return either way. I would use the five-day plan and the Savi ™ Accelerated Partial Breast Irradiation (APBI). The remembrance of how painful the mastectomy and reconstruction I'd undergone a few years earlier was what made me choose the treatment that would cause me less pain and stress.

I called the oncologist to set up a treatment schedule. She assured me that I would get through the procedure, and that she would be with me every step of the way. My surgeon would install the device in his office and then I would go to the radiation lab. I slept fitfully the night before the procedure since my breast was still sore from the partial mastectomy surgery and three previous biopsies.

The device was inserted with a local numbing solution on Friday, two days before treatment began on Monday. It was somewhat painful during the procedure, and the pain grew worse as the day wore on. The surgeon asked if I needed a prescription for pain meds, but I had some pills leftover from the earlier surgery. I declined his offer, thinking I would be okay with Tylenol, but I wasn't. I later had to resort to the pain pills I still had.

He inserted the Savi™ applicator into the cavity, and I was now ready for delivery of radiation treatments via the catheters that hung outside my breast. The Savi™ was FDA approved in 2006. It is custom-fitted to the breast regardless of what size or shape it is after surgery. The device looks like a small wire whisk but is actually a bundle of soft, tiny catheters. The Savi™ has a long handle at the end. The device is inserted flat, and after it's fitted into the cavity, it gets cranked open with a key, expanding it within the cavity.

A Savi™ representative, Susan Landsman, R.T., from Cianna Medical—the company that holds its patent-pending trademark—was there for the entire procedure. She assisted the doctor since she was an expert in custom-fitting the device. My surgeon, Dr. R., had expertise in the insertion of the applicator. Together, they used ultrasound to guide the process.

I was a bit shaken to see the Cianna rep during the procedure as no one had informed me this would be the case. I rushed home afterward to research any lawsuits on the device, but I found nothing negative. Ms. Landsman later reassured me that it was standard practice for her to assist. The doctor had to be trained and advised regarding size and other factors pertaining to the insertion of the implant. She told me that 5,000 implants had been performed since the Savi™ had been FDA approved.[2] I couldn't find many follow-up studies that dated back past five years, but I did

---

[2] Pam Stephan, About.com Guide. (Accessed March 18, 2010) http://breastcancer.about.com/od/radationtherapy/tp/savi_radiation.htm

discover that this type of device was also used for prostate, gynecological, and lung cancers.[3]

After the doctor finished, the area was cleansed, and the wound, a tiny slit, was covered by an ace bandage wound around my entire breast. I was shaky, so I was glad that I had my sister to drive me to my appointments that day.

When I got to the oncology department at the hospital, I was immediately ushered in for a CT. Sharon, the nurse, assisted me onto the table for the scan. A wide-bore CT simulator scanner was used. This new equipment was a multi-slice, computed topography scanner with specialized features that helped the doctor plan the course of treatment. The brachytherapy physicists, John and Victor, came in to meet me and take the measurements that would be fed into the computer to determine the dosage I would receive through the eleven tiny catheters of the Savi™.

Due to the location of my tumor cavity, the tiny strands were under my armpit where I couldn't see them without a mirror. My caretaker would need to clean them twice a day over the weekend following specific instructions. I received a cleaning kit. It included two front-closing bras and that I was to wear 24-7 during my radiation treatment along with the necessary cleaning materials.

I was in pain, so I didn't do much over the weekend, just read and rested. The area around the implant was painful; it oozed, and it was beginning to bruise. My angelic sister, Ananfaye, bless her, came twice a day over the weekend to clean my incision and replace the dressing.

My son brought me in for my first day of radiation the next week at 9:00 a.m. I had to have another CT scan. With some difficulty, I was maneuvered into position. The catheters hung close to my back and under my arm, so I had to roll to

---

[3] http://www.bannerhealth.com/locations/Arizona/Banner+Desert+Medical+Ce (Accessed April, 21, 2010)

the right, keep my head straight, lift my left arm over my head and contort into a side position, and then straighten myself on the table. The nurse marked me with a black marker so we could more easily arrange me in the same position for the afternoon session.

I was then wheeled into the radiation room where wires hanging from the machine that disbursed the radiation were attached to the catheters connected to my breast. John explained that it was like threading needles, so it took a few moments. The first radiation delivery consisted of a check of the catheters and a test run before the actual eight minutes of therapy. Then he and Victor went into another room where they watched me on a monitor as I was blasted with radiation.

John and Victor thoroughly explained the technology to me. My radiation oncologist was there ready to answer any other questions I had. Before each session, she checked the delivery and asked me how I was doing.

During the test portion of the procedure, it felt as though a match burned along the inside of my breast. I learned later that this was due to the use of the larger needles that were needed for that phase. The treatment itself felt like tiny pinpricks along the inside of my breast, which sent a slight pain through my nipple even though the wires and delivery weren't that close to it. My radiation dose was 34 Gy in ten fractions (3.4) over five days, twice a day. This was about half of the amount that would have been delivered during external beam radiation over a six or seven week course.

My son and I left the hospital the day after the first treatment around ten thirty. I rewarded myself with a pedicure. Riding in the car made me nauseous for the first couple of hours; however, after a long lunch the nausea was gone so I shopped at a health food store where I bought aloe vera juice to drink because it sooths burns. I visualized that it would somehow enter my breast cavity and give me relief. I also bought a large, floppy hat to wear in my convertible, since I had to avoid the sun during and after the radiation—no small feat in Arizona.

I returned for the second treatment, repeated the CT scan and the eight-minute radiation delivery, and finished about 4:00 p.m.

Each day, the nurses cleansed my wound with alcohol, applied an antibacterial gel and dressed it with gauze after both treatments, so I didn't need to clean the site at home. I could barely walk from the garage to the bedroom and fell onto the bed exhausted from the day, so my son fixed me something to eat, if I needed to, later. I ate a little, but I didn't have much appetite.

During the days that followed, I repeated the twice-daily treatments at intervals approximately six hours apart. Since the drive there was long and coincided with rush hour traffic, my son and I decided to stay in the area and run errands, laze in the shade and eat long lunches each day.

After a few days, treatment became easier, although I still felt tired and anxious to be done and home safe after a long day. The physicists would call out the four-minute mark so I would know that the treatment was half over. During each treatment, radiation was sent down one catheter at a time with different dosages given at points along the length of the catheter.

I couldn't wash my hair, so most days I tied it up with a clip to get the mess out of my face. The day my daughter-in law Trish took me we found a lovely knit cap in the waiting area that matched my turquoise purse, and I put it on to hide my unwashed hair. The caps had been made by volunteers for radiation and chemotherapy patients who had to deal with hair loss and being unable to shower for ten to fourteen days while in radiation and recovery. (I had a European showerhead, so I was able to wash myself from the waist down and do a sponge bath on the rest of my body, but I still felt dirty.)

The process had its good and bad moments. I seemed to be tolerating the dosage, and had no redness at the catheter site. Either Sharon or Sam, the nurses, would set me up both morning and afternoon for a CT scan, ensuring that the implant didn't move. I worried about all that imaging because of what my breast had already been subjected to, but I realized it was necessary. The two physicists, John and Victor, used a Geiger counter after each treatment to make sure I wasn't radioactive. It all seemed surreal and a bit scary. I asked what would happen if the radiation seed got stuck or something happened to dislodge it. Jokingly, Victor replied, "Well, then we'd all run out of the room and leave you on the table."

During one radiation treatment, I suddenly felt a burning sensation that pulsated across the top of my breast. I called out to the men. They had already stopped the machine and were entering the room. They adjusted the catheters. The radioactive seed on catheter number eight had stalled for some reason. The physicists didn't seem too concerned, and they re-started the treatment after some adjustments. After that, I didn't ask questions—no need to tempt providence.

My hair got stringy in the middle of the week. During the in-between-treatment break, my son took me to a beauty school where I had my hair washed and blown dry. I felt better mentally, if not physically. My fatigue was worse. However, I was lucky; I had three caretakers sharing my journey with me, my son and his wife, and my sister.

We stopped to pick up Chinese food for dinner. I'd had only soup and salad each day for lunch since the contortions I went through for both the CT and radiation dictated a light meal. Often, I wasn't very hungry, just thirsty beyond belief. The Chinese food tasted awful, and I couldn't eat. I drank water and aloe vera juice all night. The idea of the aloe was comforting as again, I visualized it swishing around the cavity of my burned breast even though I knew it was actually in my digestive tract. I began to see that I would complete the treatment.

The days passed slowly. Night sweats caused me to lay awake for hours and feel dragged out during the day. This was a known side effect of radiation, as was the nausea and fatigue.

By Thursday, my fourth day of treatment, the fatigue was extreme, and I could scarcely make it from the car to my bed. I craved a milkshake, so my dear sister went to McDonald's to get a chocolate shake for my dinner. I drank more water. If I drank a lot of water, I believed I could flush the radiation out of me. I knew the radioactive seeds went through me and back into the machine, but it felt like the residue was destroying other parts of my body, not just my breast. My mouth was parched, and all night I drank cool water. I noticed a red rash on my upper chest and small pimples, nowhere near the radiation site, as I readied myself for bed, but I was too tired to care. I applied aloe vera gel to the rash on my upper chest and by the next night, it was gone.

On the last day, my ninth session, I arrived in the radiation office at 8:00 a.m. I was excited because I only had two more treatments—this morning session, and the one I'd have that afternoon. The treatment went smoothly; my skin didn't redden or burn at the catheter site, and I was tired but glad to be over the hump.

Between treatments, my son and I ran a few errands and treated ourselves to a couple of chocolate samples at See's Candies. I bought a box of dark chocolates (antioxidants) for my radiation team. It was my way of saying "thank you." They were true professionals, every one of them.

When I went back for my very last treatment, number ten, I was ecstatic! Again, all went well. After the treatment, my doc took the Savi™ applicator from my breast. I felt only slight discomfort, nothing like I'd felt when they put it in.

The representative from Savi™ was in the radiation suite. She had come to assist with a new patient. I described my experience with the Savi™ to her and said that I'd definitely recommend the device to any suitable candidate. She was interested to discover that I could actually feel the radiation delivery.

Something else I began to notice during the radiation treatment was that, although I was still psychic and needed to turn it off at times, the usual bouts of illuminated information—visual or telepathic—weren't in evidence. The radiation caused disturbed sleep, but the voices were silent, so I was able to drift back off. Even my deceased mother—who would regularly communicate with me at 3:10 a.m.—uttered not a word. I believe that my gatekeeper, St. Anne of Cleves, kept the unseen entities at bay so my body could heal. Either that or the radiation itself coated me with a barrier to the spirit world for my own protection.

I was filled with gratitude that it was all over, that I had amazing doctors and access to good healthcare. Everyone hugged me. I responded with gusto, happy to be finished and to be alive. I entered the waiting area and enthusiastically rang the cowbell there to signal the end of my treatment. Everyone clapped and wished me luck. I was truly blessed!

On Saturday when I awoke I said aloud, "What a glorious day! No radiation. I got it all done in one workweek!" I took my shower (from the waist down until the wound healed). I was happy to see I still had a breast—a bit smaller from the lumpectomy, with a few scars—three to be exact, one from the removal of the tumor; one from the sentinel node removal; and a small, straight slit where the Save™ applicator had been inserted. It would heal with time and the scars would fade. I was still me.

I recalled the surgeon telling me when I'd had my mastectomy that my right breast would be like Swiss cheese if he tried to save it, and I thought about how far I had come since then. Now I knew that I'd have taken even the Swiss cheese breast if that had been my only option, so long as I would live.

My joy knew no bounds. The melancholy was gone. I was excited about the possibilities for the rest of my life. I was grateful there would be life to come.

Chapter 20
2011 – Possibilities

My life had a new norm now. Living with cancer, for me, meant living in present time, a lesson I thought I'd learned once before but somehow forgot. My second bout of cancer had taken me away, temporarily, from my practice of "bending time."

I had read Stuart Wilde's book, *The Quickening*, when it was first published in the 1980s. His idea of slowing time to accomplish more without feeling stressed was something I readily incorporated. The trick was to expand time by mentally deciding that I had enough of it. At first, I had to pretend that I had all the time in the world, that I wasn't busy or rushed, and slowly, I learned to stay in the moment, second by second.

The practitioner can see how amazing this technique is when it becomes part of one's daily habit. I began to bend my perception of time, and the spatial quality widened and changed. I worked on expanding time so I could fit more into my schedule. I found out the way to do that was to cherish each second as if it was the only time I had left and stay in the moment, which lengthened and heightened each experience. What I was left with was the extraordinary feeling that there was no limit to how much I could accomplish in any given time period.

Later, I read Eckhart Tolle's, *The Power of Now*, and his words I never forgot: "Nothing ever happened in the past; it happened in the Now. Nothing will ever happen in the future; it will happen in the Now." These seemed like odd words for a psychic to remember given that I made my living by reading the past, present, and future. My clients told me I was "predictive," so the "future" was my forte. Yet my life was all about the now.

The second diagnosis of cancer scared me out of this mode into fretting about the future, and I was forced to look at the same issues all over again. Slowly, I began the task of bending time anew. I stayed in the present, and, with some practice, I felt balanced and at peace once more.

However, this time around, the revitalization of my life felt different. There was an urgency to live in a way that I had never before experienced. Not only did I need to re-examine my health issues, but I had to deal with my fears. At first I felt out of control, and that I was being twisted by the aberrant whims of the health gods.

All around me, the world was in chaos, yet focusing inward to seize a quiet state within my core of knowingness, I found harmony. My spiritual renewal energized me in new ways, and I began to think about the "four paths of creation" spirituality that I had encountered while reading the writings of Matthew Fox. Fox, building on Meister Eckhart's mystical vision, identified four major ways that people connect to divinity both in and beyond the physical world. The first two paths are of ways of **being**, while the second two are ways of **doing**. The first path, the **Via Positiva**, is a means by which we encounter divinity through experiences of awe and delight, wonder and astonishment in the world and universe around us enjoying life's basic gifts. As Matthew Fox noted in *Creation* the Via Positiva suggests; "Thou shalt fall in love at least three times a day." The second path, the **Via Negativa**, is encountering divinity by embracing our shadow and experiencing our dark side through the experiences of loss, of suffering and letting go, and in our darkness embrace excesses, allowing the pain to be pain. The third path, the **Via Creativa**, is meeting divinity through creative activity, totally expressing our true selves through art as a form of meditation. The fourth path, the **Via Transformativa**, is becoming an agent of divinity by using one's creative energy to transform self and society through acts of compassion, justice and wisdom. The four paths are interconnected; they are like the facets of a light, on a sparkling gemstone. Thus, experiences of joy and sorrow can inspire artistry and activism and come close to the bliss of peace and wonder.

Fox's controversial teachings in contravention with the Roman Catholic Church beliefs were his idea that we are born into "original blessing" (the name of one of his books) rather than as the Catholic Church taught that we are born into "original sin." Also, he taught the four paths of creation spirituality rather than the church's teachings of classical purgation, illumination and union. He further gained attention from Rome when he called God "Mother" and worked too closely with Native America spiritual practices, and did not condemn homosexuality. In 1993, Fox's continued conflicts with his church ended with his expulsion from the Dominican order ending his professional relationship with the church and his teachings at Catholic universities.

I identified with the spiritual journey of Matthew Fox particularly because he had once been a Dominican Catholic priest in California, and when he began to formulate his secular theories, the Church ex-communicated him, so he left the priesthood. The Episcopal Church received him with open arms when this happened, and he became an Episcopalian priest.

I felt as though I had experienced aspects of each of the four paths, and I began to look at the world around me, aware that my spiritual renewal was synchronistic with The Awakening in the Middle East.

My son Barry and I went to Egypt in late 2009. At that time, there wasn't an inkling of what was to come in Cairo. We enjoyed the marvelous Pyramids at Giza and took a cruise along the Nile as we consumed a delicious dinner and were entertained by whirling dervishes and belly dancers. We stayed at the luxurious Mena House, one of the famous

Oberoi Hotels near the Pyramids and strolled along Tahrir Square. We visited the Egyptian Museum nearby and ate in the cafes along what would become Revolution Road.

We left, and, within a few weeks, tourists fled the city. Protestors against the regime made their voices heard. However, as with all spiritual and political upheaval, the country and its people paid a price. They lost their jobs, the tourists left, and the government turned on its own citizens. Who would have imagined that a prodemocracy movement fostered by social media would oust Hosini Mubarak, the President of Egypt?

In 2005, activists organized a group called "Youth for Change." However, because they tried to work through established channels, they never accomplished what they had originally set out to do. Their quest was to end the twenty-three year long state of emergency that had enabled Mubarak to stay in power. These student activists were media-savvy, well-traveled, and were often seen meeting in cafes with their coffees, laptops and hubble-bubble pipes, eager to live their slogan, "Kifaya," Arabic for "Enough."

Again, in 2008, the group tried to organize labor strikes but the police cracked down on them with brutal tactics. During our visit to Alexandria, Egypt, the following year, garbage with a stench that gagged us littered the streets. Sanitation workers hadn't picked it up in weeks due to an attempted strike and continuing labor unrest.

The mass protests that erupted in Egypt began with the inner turmoil each individual must have endured prior to the decision to speak out against the government. When bullets whizzed around them in Cairo, had they suffered anguished moments of doubt? Had they wondered whether they'd made the right choice? I identified with their ways of thinking and their willingness to risk everything because of the possibilities that might be revealed on an individual and collective basis. Some must have had arguments with their families as they made the choice to stay home from work—

which put their family members at risk. They faced bullets, death or arrest, and still they fought with sticks and stones against soldiers with tanks, guns, and knives. They didn't know what would happen, yet they persisted in the face of great odds.

Unexpectedly, in January 2011, the protestors found an ally in Wael Ghonim, an Egyptian executive working in Dubai as head of Google marketing for the Mid-East and North Africa. He set up a Facebook group named for Khalid Mohamed Said, the young Egyptian who had been beaten to death by police in Alexandria in June, 2010 under suspicious circumstances.

Wael's compelling words on his facebook wall—"We are all Khalid"—attracted hundreds of thousands of followers. His activism incited over 100,000 protestors to attend rallies in Tahrir Square and elsewhere. A Buddhist proverb states, "When the student is ready, the master appears." Students—young and old—in Egypt were ready. Dictatorship in this modern world no longer belonged in the realm of possibility.

After a period of constant protests, disappearances and bloodshed that began on January 25, 2011, Mubarak finally abdicated rulership on February 11, 2011. The military stepped forward and took power. The new rulers recently announced an interim constitution to replace the one that was suspended when Mubarak stepped down.

The power of social media cannot be denied. Was a network of idealists who believed that all things are possible the catalyst for social change? Or was the catalyst simply everyday students and workers who'd had "Enough" and were energized by the world they dreamed of, their own seemingly impossible dream?

Political upheaval, like spiritual awakening, teaches those involved "something different is possible." Was it this social media, or the hero, Wael Ghonim, who awakened Egyptians to the option of living a different life? In the words of one Egyptian man, "I never thought this was possible. I have lived my whole life in fear." An elderly man on the streets of Cairo said, "I will never go back to that way of living again. Give me freedom now or let me die!"

The Buddha put it this way, "All things come and go, but the awakened awake forever." Until humans embrace possibility thinking, we can't lift depression, or gain insight, or act in extraordinary ways. Political and spiritual insights created possibilities for the Egyptians. They were finally able to see that Egypt, too, could claim the kind of life that's experienced in Europe or the United States.

Unfortunately, my mother, who clinically depressed and unreasonably anxious, saw suicide as her only viable option because she was too sick to envision any other possibility. Possibility thinking is the opposite of my mother's despair; it moves us forward and frees us from the demons of cynical, negative thinking.

My failed attempts to practice law in the manner I envisioned; the deaths of both my parents (especially the trauma of Mother's suicide); divorce; law school anomalies, difficult teenagers; unrelenting, unwanted psychic visions; plus a cross-country move that almost rendered me unable to see my own possibilities were all barriers that could have shattered my psyche. However, I chose the possibility that I was truly a medium, and that I could and should embrace the real me.

When I finally told a select few friends about my bizarre experience aboard a spacecraft, I had almost stopped envisioning the possible. I could have chosen to see my abduction experience as an imaginative dream, or a transcendental journey like that of a mystic or shaman who returns in spiritual rebirth. I could have viewed it the way C.G. Jung did when he posited a "new mythology of Flying Saucers." Or, I could have assumed I was mentally ill— hallucinatory, or worse, psychotic. Instead, I chose to create the possibility in my mind of extraterrestrial life, research the subject, join MUFON (Mutual UFO Network), and follow the latest UFO research for the rest of my adult life.

I identified strongly with those who participated in the Egyptian uprising and those in the countries that followed suit. I still felt beaten down by my second cancer surgery and the aftermath of radiation treatment. But watching the courage of the Egyptians, how they faced their demons in order to change and move forward, energized and healed me completely.

I had conquered cancer, twice, and it was a formidable enemy. Cancer definitely changed all perceptions I'd previously held about myself. Now, no longer caring about the person I was, or what is in the past, I look forward to all the possibilities that my new life has to offer. The first step in discovering a new possibility is to search for it; my search is for the next possibility that will enable me to discover anew what I can do and who I can be.

One of my prayers upon awakening each morning is to ask God to send me clients—if and only if—it is in alignment with my soul's continued journey. Each time I move from city to city or visit country to country, I am called on to do readings that heal those who are in need. I always travel with a small recording device so they can play back the session. This encourages them to heed the advice of their own spirit guides who can reveal the secrets of their destiny.

But is this enough? What other things are possible for me? I thrive upon the energy of my clients and all those who follow my website and my postings on Facebook, Twitter and other social media. At this juncture in my life, what more am I to do? With the waning of the moon, I leave the autumn of my life and ready myself for the winter of my existence. Yet, inside I feel as though I'm more akin to the souls whose inner stirrings created the Arab spring.

We live in tumultuous times, caught as we are in the midst of a paradigm shift that will alter our thought patterns.

Things never change by themselves, but rather adjust as they are driven by outside forces. As we have seen in the Middle East, the new communication technologies can become the catalysts for change. The cell phone, the laptop and the Internet, all fueled by human imagination are creating limitless possibilities both in our personal lives and in our business endeavors. We are shifting from a mechanistic, manufacturing society to a service-based, information-centered society that is eager for the truths of spiritual peace. We are no longer the post-industrial society we once were.

I, too, am changing as I move at an accelerated rate of consciousness, transforming and transcending. I consider the gifts I possess to include the elements of the Triad of the Goddess. I am The Young Maiden as I learn new technological and communication skills every day in order to grow and continue to convey my message. I am The Mother to my adult children and a Mother to the bewildered, confused, and anxious as they awaken to their own soul's journey. I am The Crone, old enough to be proficient as a Seer, wise and aware of my own unique skill set. I have surmounted many obstacles in my lifetime to heed my call to service, and I humbly acknowledge that I've begun to master The Crone's aged wisdom.

In what new ways am I to use these gifts? What now is possible?

What if *all* things are possible?

Afterword: Ascension
Sedona, Arizona: March 27, 2027

I am a Seer. That is what I do.

What I see before me is a possibility.

Although I believe that it's not impossible to change the vision I relate below, it can only be done with focused world co-operation.

My decision has been made to leave planet Earth. Our squadron is prepared and the orders have been given to proceed. I am ready. Prior to my incarnation in this lifetime, I made a service agreement with the Intergalactic Guardians of Soul Retrieval, and I long to fulfill my destiny. My husband, Gared, and my grown children have also committed to the Ascension.

The vibrational frequency of my physical body and my etheric body are in alignment. I must return to the planet I have come from, Pleiades. As a humanoid, I have a shared ancestry with the Pleiadians who originated on Venus. Resources are exhausted regionally in my family's desert terrain and will soon be depleted throughout the planet. The Galactic Federation has determined that the Nano technology for human transfer is now perfected, therefore; the time is now for the exodus. Due to the critical lack of water, the population cannot survive if the shortage remains at current levels. Governing bodies of the Galactic Federation sought new solutions, but the secret alliances of world leaders with a lust for power and money blocked efforts toward the desired cooperation between earthling and extraterrestrial civilizations.

Potable water on our planet is almost gone. Fossil fuel use only increased the level of greenhouse gases. Instead, nuclear desalination has been used more in the last twenty years throughout the world with the Middle East, China and Africa building plants using the energy-intensive reverse osmosis techniques. Competing countries rather than world co-operation split the growth between individual countries and the services offered by the UN's (IAEA) International Atomic Energy Agency. The huge demand should have encompassed longer-term goals using hydrogen conversion techniques. Why were we not prepared?

Greenpeace warned against catastrophes like the nuclear disaster in Japan at the Fukushima Daiichi nuclear plant, in 2011. They predicted it would cause long-term destruction and contaminate the food supply as well as the fish in the Pacific Ocean. This has unfortunately come to pass. Japanese public officials disseminated propaganda that Japan would return to normal within a year. However, food shortages due to radiation contamination were followed by famine. Global leaders stuck in the old world paradigm of three-dimensional thinking couldn't make the shift necessary to cross the threshold into new ways of possibility thinking and shared global technology.

We as Brothers and Sisters of the Federation understand the necessity for the transport since our earth's population has experienced devastating water shortages, destructive wars, erratic tectonic plate changes, climate manipulation by hostile enemies, famines, and shortages of precious fuel.

China is one major case in point. It put no controls on pollutants in both the rural areas and the cities, especially Beijing, where chemical dumping in the rural areas leached in and contaminated the city's water supply. The unchecked corruption of its leaders made it necessary for them to colonize Mars for a safer environment much earlier than expected. The chastened Chinese have established settlements on the red planet. Their advanced technology is amazing. They have extracted oxygen and hydrogen from the ice on Mars and have utilized it for rocket fuel.

The survivalists, cosmologists and scientists who stay on Earth must now prioritize the stewardship of our remaining resources. As a Lightrunner™ (the trademark I have coined to identify myself because I am called to run the Light throughout the world), I feared this departure, thinking it wasn't possible to achieve so quickly.

Our space flight today is with Virgin Galactic, a company that remains at the forefront of commercial space flights since their first mothership, Eve, was created. As the safest and most popular Space-line, they have accelerated research at an incredible rate by joining with corporate America to create aircrafts. Thus, they were able to spend money that NASA (National Aeronautics and Space Administration) couldn't justify due to budget issues. Further, their bold partnership with extraterrestrial life forms—sharing technology and learning new scientific thought patterns—has compelled them to excel. Hybrid scientists and aeronautical experts from Earth made space travel to Pleiades possible by committing to interstellar cooperation.

The people from the Pleiades cluster traveled in the past by a process similar to a hologram whereby the images were telepathically transmitted for viewing through an optical camouflage. The future, it appears, is in programmable matter, which already exists in some forms where atoms have been replaced by chips. Others in the galaxy have, with a simple click of a cursor, changed soft to hard, paper to stone, and have gone from super fluorescent to super reflective to invisible.

UFO incidents written off as impossible occurrences in the past—such as shapeshifting crafts with stealth capabilities invisible to radar or crafts that suddenly appeared through some sort of portal—all now have valid scientific explanations. Earth scientists gained the tools of these new sciences via cooperation with extraterrestrial beings. Since the public disclosure and release of evidence supporting claims that our government has been working with extraterrestrial life forms, our citizens assumed that our scientists back-engineered UFO-type crafts and were capable of interstellar access. They tried to do this earlier to no avail. They learned that spaceships must be constructed from the ground up by beginning with the necessary science. This has taken years to accomplish.

The only reason we earthlings have come to understand the science upon which the new technologies are based is because extraterrestrial visitors have shared their technology with us in order that we might leave our rocket method of propulsion behind. Therefore, we have had to embrace revisions in our scientific theories in order to see that new possibilities existed. The long-held belief was that an extraterrestrial craft could not come from other parts of the universe because the speed of light made it impossible. We now know that is not true.

As we began to create monopoles in our laboratories, we thought that with enough monopoles, our ships would float through space pulled along by the magnetic field lines found throughout the galaxy or on individual planets. Again we met with failure. However, there exist other magnetic influences in the galaxy that have been harnessed by extraterrestrial beings whose technology we are just now beginning to understand. What we once considered impossible was simply lack of knowledge, and now we are able, with their help, to travel through space magnetically.

Beamships are used for mass human transport or extraterrestrial visitations for the purpose of gathering information and observation of humans.

During our time aboard Eve, our Captain will be in constant contact with the Pleiadians who will monitor our trip via communication from their star planet. Other Federation members located on the Moon base will also observe. Nearby, on Mars, the Chinese Federation of Mars (CFM) physicists and cosmologists will be on call, as well. Galactic Federation members within the occupied solar system are in contact with the remaining Earth scientists from SETI (Search for Extraterrestrial Intelligence).

Construction by the Chinese on Mars has been remarkable. They have used advanced alien technology coupled with their own advancements to create useful magnet shields and fabrics that reflect radiation (like Demron). The Mars occupants have also managed to create artificial gravity, establish food and water supplies, and integrate life support systems. Many westerners attended school in China and have been trained through the Mars Advocacy community in China. They will be able to teach diverse skill sets to other émigrés when they reach their new environment. They returned with their families to America specifically for the Ascension relocation.

I will have plenty of time to muse on the past, wondering what as a nation we could have done to prevent this moment in time. However, the present calls me to reality and the moment of Ascension.

I stand at the head of the coalition poised for the transfer from the red rocks of Sedona onto the ships that will arrive within the next few hours. The vortexes of Sedona hold this sacred landing space open with their funnels of spiraling energy. Cathedral Rock has a mild vortex while the creek waters of Oak Creek and Red Rock Crossing are strongest where you walk east along the creek toward Cathedral Rock. It is hard to believe in this desert terrain and drought that Juniper trees still stand, though the creek bed is dry.

This departure is being re-enacted throughout the world in other sacrosanct desert areas where extreme heat has depleted the water supply and made them uninhabitable. The Sahara Desert League Coalition members are evacuating émigré's from the Middle East at this time. They will meet us at our destination.

Global members of the Central Federation Agency (CFA) have coordinated with Regional Council heads, Ascended Masters of Wisdom, and local Galactic Federation representatives. All are ready to assist the feeble, the elderly and the children in remaining calm when they exit the crafts at our destination.

As I look around, I am chronologically senior to many of the people around me. I am confident that as we transfer from planet Earth, the completion of our ascension consciousness will move us immediately through new dimensional frequencies at a rapid rate and beyond.

The desert queue today is filled with young folks and plenty of children. The sun is hot and each man, woman and child wears a helmet and clothes made of Sunaja fabrics designed to protect every surface of their bodies from the sun. Any exposed skin is sealed with aloe glaze. Protective facemasks reflect off the blazing sun to keep it from burning our eyes and lips.

My son, Barry, and my daughter, Sheila, along with their families, stand beside me, prepared to load the émigrés onto the ships that have landed. My husband waits for me nearby. He said to me this morning, "We might change our minds and choose to ascend without our bodies."

I smile at him, knowing we will ascend in our bodies. "Yes dear. We will see." My vision is clear. We will die in our current bodies on Pleiades. For now, I go with what has been foretold to me. I don't intend to stay in this heat without water, and I don't intend to live underground like the survivalists who have chosen to remain on Earth. I will return to Pleiades, and I will die with my family at my side.

We are carrying only enough water for the trip, but the cosmologists assure us that the liquid readily available on Pleiades will tide us over until we can grow our own protein and convert it to liquid matter. This substance, when misted into our mouths, is comparable to water due to the atmospheric elements on Pleiades that immediately convert the compound when combined with our saliva.

The main source of protein eaten on Pleiades comes from a plant that grows above ground and looks like spinach. It is leafy and green and has a rapid growth cycle. The leaves and vines can be boiled, stewed, or dehydrated. Once harvested, it is dried into powder and enriched with a soy-like ingredient mixed with synthetic vitamins and minerals. It contains ingredients that produce more protein-building enzymes within our bodies than anything known on Earth.

The Federation has provided a cache of the product on the craft for us, if needed. Pleiadians eat only once every two weeks, consuming 8.5 milliliters at a time. They have no weight variations. They don't consume through their mouths but instead use an instrument like a tuning fork to inhale the powdered substance through their noses. Because their nostrils are flat to their faces rather than protruding, the food substance is easily tipped into the cavity.

Besides the green substance, they produce a sweet berry that looks like a cranberry but tastes entirely different. It is grown in hothouses and is pulverized and inhaled as a change from their diet of the green soy powder. (I wonder if my children will learn to produce their beloved veggie burgers on Pleiades.)

The molecular structure of the oxygen on Earth is similar to Pleiades. By administering themselves with a serum, Pleiadians are able to spend time on Earth working with the earthlings who have made Karmic agreements with them.

Experimentation on Pleiades with abductees has proved that, with a little assistance, our Earth bodies will adapt until a new generation of hybrids can be genetically designed. Due to the previously inconceivable electrical and physical changes in our cellular makeup, as well as great changes in our collective consciousness over the last fifty years, many leaders have been trained for the transport and the integration into Pleiadian life.

Some breeding between the species occurred due to seeding during earthling abductions, but sexual intercourse played no part in the reproduction. Our DNA and RNA are similar to that of the Pleiadians. It took many experimental attempts in order to successfully spawn progeny. Resulting hybrids from these experiments are scattered among us. They are scientists and healers known as Lightworkers and Lightrunners. Genetically, the progeny have a much higher intelligence than Earth humanoids, and they engage in telepathy unparalleled to that of normal humans.

In addition, the terra-forming of Pleiades is being adapted to meet the needs of the first Earth settlers. Domed structures for habitation in the biosphere, greenhouses, manufacturing workspaces and pressurized rovers for exploration are already in place for our use.

This journey home is the culmination of my life's work. My service mission has been to develop my higher consciousness and skill set to teach everyone I meet to "see" like I do. I have been told that I change people's lives with my gifts of prophesy and vision, but I do not change people's lives; they change their own lives. Spirit speaks through me, compelling their truth to the surface of their consciousness so they may speak it aloud and clear whilst owning their own dreams.

A Seer's vision, the Pleiadians say, is science, based on degrees of probability. Galactic motivation for visitation and communication with us has been an attempt to align us with the means to save our resources in a timely fashion and forego the destruction of our planet. All that has been foretold has happened. Was no one listening? Our seas and lands remain polluted, the air we breathe filled with toxins. Some efforts to conserve our forestland and cultivate our oceans occurred, but we failed to dispose of nuclear waste adequately or take responsibility for updating our nuclear plants. We also continued storing dangerous chemicals underground or dumped them into the ocean.

Today, as we board the craft, I can say that I was instrumental in orchestrating this great event. I transmitted messages from intergalactic masters for the Federation Elders as they were given to me. The messages revealed the plan for our exodus and the dissemination of this information globally. I have worked hard to become the galactic human I was meant to be. I am proud to head the coalition.

I look out across the mesa upon the red rock monoliths and sense the fears of an old gentleman, standing in line, shriveled and dried up from the heat. He holds a small leather pouch filled with flint for making fire—why, I don't know. He caresses the stone with his fingers lovingly. I walk closer to him.

"We will need fire, I think," he says to me.

A small dog jumps at his heels. Has no one told him that pets can't be taken at this time? The High Council of the Federation agreed unanimously— no pets. Some species may be transported in the next round, but no personal pets for now.

Later, animals for reproduction and healthy pets will come to Pleiades from the moon in unmanned reconnaissance crafts via tethered space elevators, after their body temperatures have been lowered until bodily functions cease through suspended animation techniques. When they arrive, a cadre of specialists at the Moon base will retrieve them from the crafts and revive them. The Chinese Intergalactic Federation along with the Russian Intergalactic Federation at the Moon base will take responsibility for their security throughout the thawing process. Then each animal will be sent on to Pleiades where they will greet their owners in perfect health.

Ashi is the Federation's Operational Director and I see he is standing near a stunted Ocotillo tree. I walk over to him and whisper for him to relay the message privately to those with pets that they can't be boarded. He stares down at his dry, cracked desert boots, unable to look directly at me. I know he wishes I would give the command via my own implanted earphone so he would not have to spread the news. Stone-faced, Ashi carries out my orders. He assures the owners that their animals will be teleported to the mountains or an underground site, with a group of survivalists who will gladly care for them until we are settled. He tugs his ear, mouthing a code to include only animal owners in the communication as he transmits this information through his implanted communication device, and soon the air is filled with anguished cries from the pet owners. I can barely look at the old man as his eyes flood with tears, yet I cannot see them roll down his face behind his mask. He kisses his small border collie on her snout and pats her head. His wizened tanned hand ruffles through her long furry coat.

Ashi begins to reorganize the lines of passengers to make sure that families board together so they can share their allotment of food and water for the journey.

Peering upward, the crowd watches the Beamships before they land soundlessly on the desert floor close to Oak Creek Canyon, on a landing pad of red rocked mesa. Silently, the crowd arranges itself into a single queue. From my angled vision, Cathedral Rock juts above us showing one of her many faces and I see my children with their families move closer to the landing site. The Native Americans called Cathedral Rock "Sun God" as its rosy scarlet glow is especially beautiful at sunset and sunrise. It is almost sunset and I am reminded of this image as the desert cloaks itself in scarlet.

My heart is heavy. Life has been good on planet Earth, and I am sad to leave it. Leaving my home is difficult and I know that all of us here share the same fears. The desert is hot and arid but familiar to us as Arizonians. The sunflowers, the yucca, cholla and the agave appear to sustain life in this extreme heat. The Coconino National Forest surrounds us though some of the greenery is charred and the white Oaks are no longer prevalent.

I take in the smell and particles of dust, but also notice a faint whiff of sweet desert flowers.

My husband has finally reached me from his place at the end of the line, and I place my staff in the soil beside him as we enter the Beamship. I turn to acknowledge the Commander and he calls out.

"Susan, I knew you would be here."

"How many light years do we travel, Commander?" I ask as he greets me.

"Faster than the speed of thought," he answers. There is always some error in these travel calculations. We may stop at the Moon base for supplies and fueling.

The Russians leisurely settled the moon while participants in the US, NASA's constellation program in 2011 with the new Orion spacecraft and Ares rocket and began testing the Orion but without funding the program came to a standstill. Other nations quickly stepped up to the race. The Galactic Federation and the United Nations begged for global cooperation in setting up a fueling depot on the moon. They tried to form a centralist organization for global co-ordination of space exploration but the cooperation was short-lived. The cooperation of the ISS (International Space Station) worked well as a multinational project, however the legal and financial aspects created monumental challenges since the treaty was signed in 1998.

The Russians have long been the leaders in low Earth orbit space. One clause in the treaty allowed RKA's ('Russian Federal Space Agency') Russian cosmonauts the right to nearly one-half of the crew time for ISS. This time allotment propelled the Russians to colonize the moon almost ten years ago without incident. The Exopolitics Institute predicted that China would get to the moon first, but Russia leapt ahead. The vision of the Exopolitics Institute wavered as they struggled to disseminate extraterrestrial science and technology in too slow of a manner.

Russians eliminated the difficult dust problem and set up habitats for colonization much sooner than expected using their amazing lunar lander and rovers.

The large Beamship filled with Americans is ready for takeoff. I tell the commander, "Dan, you're the expert. I leave the navigation to you." I recognize him from when he was a commercial airline pilot. I knew him in Miami where he worked for Eastern Airlines long ago. I feel secure because I know that he, as a Federation Elder, has handpicked his young pilots—the captain and first officer. I trust Dan's wisdom will prevail in any difficulties and will get us safely through the galaxy.

I look out the door before the guardian shuts it to make sure no one is left behind.

Now the sealing of the craft is complete, and I check the lounge of the ship and see that several women are crying and clutching their children. I hear the singsong tones of Chinese being spoken by the scientists and others who have lived in China for years but have now returned to reunite in the United States with their extended families for the exodus. The Captain announces our ascent into space and all heads bow with hands clasped. Elder Dan speaks after the Captain has given instructions for the flight. "This is Elder Dan from the flight deck. Rest in peace, Planet Earth."

Namaste.

Therefore it is.

"Oh! How I dreamt of things impossible."
- William Blake (1757-1827)

Pictured here are, from left to right,
sisters Noreen, Molly, Margaret, Gloria on the stool,
and Susan.

Susan welcomes readers who wish to connect. One way to do this is by clicking Blog and Travel on her website, www.susanstockton.com.
There, you can leave a comment, or share posts you resonate with on Facebook, Twitter, LinkedIn, Google+ or Pinterest.

www.ingramcontent.com/pod-product-compliance
Lightning Source LLC
Chambersburg PA
CBHW051420090426
42737CB00014B/2761